THE COLD WAR

THE COLD WAR

THE RISE AND FALL OF THE SOVIET UNION

TED GOTTFRIED

ILLUSTRATED BY MELANIE REIM

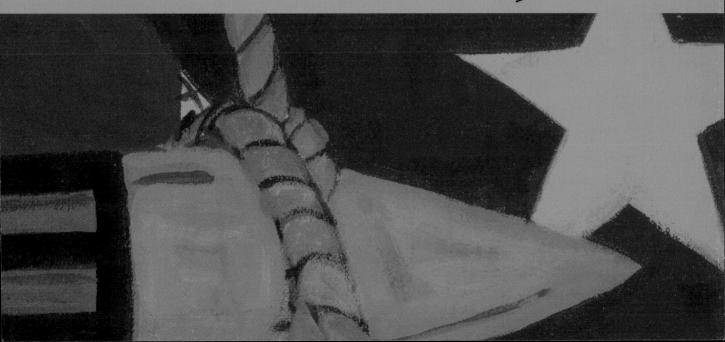

For Harriet,
with all my love

Acknowledgments
I am grateful to personnel of the New York Central Research Library, the Mid-Manhattan Library, the Society Library in New York City, and the Queensboro Public Library for aid in gathering material for this book. Also, gratitude is due my editor, Laura Walsh. While her cooperation during the writing of this series was invaluable, any shortcomings are mine alone.

Ted Gottfried

Photographs courtesy of AP/Wide World Photos: pp. 21, 69, 74, 116, 129; Getty Images: p. 33 (Hulton/Archive); Brown Brothers: p. 38; © Bettmann/Corbis: pp. 44, 63, 91, 100; Magnum Photos: pp. 54 (© Marc Riboud), 82 (© 1958 Seymour Raskin), 106. Map by Joe LeMonnier.

Library of Congress Cataloging-in-Publication Data
Gottfried, Ted.
The Cold War / Ted Gottfried ; illustrations by Melanie Reim.
p. cm.
Summary: Focuses on Soviet politics in the period between the end of World War II and the collapse of the Union of Soviet Socialist Republics (USSR), known as the Cold War.
Includes bibliographical references and index.
ISBN 0-7613-2560-3 (lib. bdg.)
1. Cold War—Juvenile literature. 2. World politics—1945—Juvenile literature. 3. Soviet Union—Foreign relations—1945-1991—Juvenile literature. [1. Cold War. 2. Soviet Union—Foreign relations—1945-1991. 3. World politics.] I. Title.
D843 .G67 2003   947.084—dc21   2002007700

Published by Twenty-First Century Books
A Division of The Millbrook Press, Inc.
2 Old New Milford Road
Brookfield, Connecticut 06804
www.millbrookpress.com

CONTENTS

A R C T I C

Svalbard

GREAT
BRITAIN

NORTH SEA

NORWAY

*Franz
Josef Lan*

BELGIUM   NETHERLANDS

DENMARK

SWEDEN

● Murmansk

*Novaya
Zemlya*

W. GERMANY

FINLAND

BARENTS SEA

KARA SEA

E. GERMANY

BALTIC SEA

● Archangel

CZECHOSLAVAKIA

POLAND

Leningrad

L. Onega

N. Dvina R.

U R A L   M T N S.

Novy Port

YUGOSLAVIA

HUNGARY

● Minsk

Smolensk ●

Dnieper R.

Moscow ✪

Don R.

Oka R.

Volga R.

Ob R.

● Berezov

ROMANIA

Kiev ●

UKRAINE
Dnepropetrovsk ●

● Kazan

Ekaterinburg ●

Ob R.

BULGARIA

Odessa ●

Crimea

Volga R.

● Samara

U N I O N   O F   S O V I E T

Sebastopol ●

BLACK SEA

Rostov ●

● Stalingrad

● Orenburg

● Omsk

TURKEY

CAUCASUS MTS.

Astrakhan ●

CASPIAN SEA

● Ekibastuz

Batum ●

● Karaganda

SYRIA

ARAL
SEA

● Kazalinsk

Baku ●

● Perovsk

IRAQ

Krasnovodsk ●

Tashkent ●

JORDAN

Ashkhabad ●

Andizhan ●

KUWAIT

IRAN

Merv ●

Samarkand ●

ARABIA

Kushka ●

AFGHANISTAN

O C E A N

BERING SEA

EAST SIBERIAN SEA

LAPTEV SEA

Anadyr

Ambarchik

Nizhnekolymsk

Kolyma R.

Nordvik

Magadan

Petropavlosk

Kamchatka
Peninsula

Okhotsk

SEA OF
OKHOTSK

Dudinka

Lena R.

S I B E R I A

Arctic Circle

Yakutsk

Viluisk

angazeia

Turukhansk

Yenisey R.

Tura

Aldan

Sakhalin
Island

Nikolaevsk

Trans-Siberian Railway,
completed in 1917

Amur R.

Angara R.

Khabarovsk

SOCIALIST REPUBLICS

Lake
Baikal

JAPAN

Tomsk

Krasnoyarsk

Bratsk

Cheremkhovo
Irkutsk

Nerchinsk

Kara

SEA
OF
JAPAN

Oka R.

MANCHURIA

Vladivostok

MONGOLIA

N. KOREA

SOVIET UNION
AND ITS
SATELLITES,
1950s-1980s

········· Iron Curtain

S. KOREA

0   300 miles

0   450 kilometers

C H I N A

PREFACE

The Cold War was the period between the end of World War II and the collapse of the Union of Soviet Socialist Republics (USSR). It consisted of a series of confrontations between the United States and the Soviet Union and their various allies and satellites. It was marked by an escalating arms race, a competition to conquer space, a dangerously belligerent form of diplomacy known as brinkmanship, and a series of small wars sometimes called "police actions" by the United States and sometimes excused as defense measures by the Soviets.

For the Soviet Union, the Cold War involved the spread of communism, the control by Moscow of other Communist nations, and the obedience of all Communists in the USSR and elsewhere to the authority of the Soviet Communist party. This book examines the USSR during the Cold War, its internal and external conflicts, and its eventual breakdown. It is also important to understand its relations with the United States during that period.

A SEESAW RELATIONSHIP

In 1939 the Soviets signed a pact with Adolf Hitler and joined the Nazis in the conquest of Poland. This aroused anti-Communist sentiment in America. Many so-called fellow travelers who had been allied with

Communists in pro-labor causes, campaigns for racial equality, battles for civil liberties, and other reforms, now scrambled to distance themselves from communism. Many members of the American Communist party left it in protest of the Nazi-Soviet alliance. Now, one could not be both anti-Nazi and for the Soviet Union.

Attitudes changed following Germany's 1941 attack on the USSR and the United States' involvement in World War II. Now, because Germany was our enemy, the Soviet Union was our ally. Politicians made speeches in favor of the Soviets. Hollywood made movies glorifying them. Pro-Soviet films like *The North Star* and *Mission to Moscow* created support among Americans. Women and children raised money for Russian war relief. The media were filled with stories of Soviet sacrifice and heroism. The Soviet dictator Joseph Stalin was now "Uncle Joe."

Then the war ended, and—abruptly—Uncle Joe was the devil and the Soviet Union was the enemy. There was good reason. Stalin was persecuting Soviet ethnic populations like the Chechens, the Balkars, and the Islamic Karachais. He was brutally stamping out democracy in the Communist satellite countries conquered in the war.

At the same time, Communists were taking over in China and Yugoslavia. In Greece and Italy there were Communist attempts to seize power. Communism was on the march and democracy was fighting a holding action.

THE COMMUNIST THREAT

Communism had been in place in the Soviet Union and had been a growing threat to the rest of the world since the Bolshevik Revolution of 1917. The Bolsheviks (literally, "those of the majority") were led by Vladimir Lenin. They promoted the extreme brand of socialism defined by Karl Marx and Friedrich Engels in *The Communist Manifesto*, first published as a pamphlet in London in 1848. The *Manifesto* proclaimed the necessity of class struggle between oppressors (all employers) and oppressed (workers). It viewed the world as two hostile camps, dismissed patriotism as a tool of capitalism, and claimed that the only loyalty workers should have was to the working class.

After the Bolsheviks, soon to be known as Communists, took over, two things happened. Lenin imposed government ownership of all property with all the military might at his command. However, when this led to widespread famine, he was forced to compromise Marxist principles and allow some individual land ownership and limited free enterprise. This program was known as the New Economic Policy (NEP).

After Lenin died in 1924, Joseph Stalin established himself as dictator of the Soviet Union. In 1928 he did away with the NEP and government ownership was reestablished. He brutally used the secret police to enforce so-called pure communism. Mass murders and widespread famine followed. By Stalin's own reckoning, some ten million people died during this period.

By the time the Soviet Union entered World War II in June 1941, Stalin's tyranny over his people was absolute. When the war ended, he extended that tyranny over the nations of Eastern Europe. His clear goal was worldwide revolution ending in Communist domination under the rule of Joseph Stalin. The threat was very real. The response was understandably extreme.

INVESTIGATING HOLLYWOOD

In the United States, anti-Communist sentiment escalated. First the government, and then various companies, required employees to sign loyalty oaths. Teachers had to account for their political views and past associations. Books considered Communist propaganda were banned from libraries.

In the entertainment industry, lists were drawn up of actors, directors, and others who had supported allegedly Communist causes. These were known as blacklists, and those whose names were on them could not get work. A past performance for Russian war relief, a wartime script sympathetic to the Soviets, and support of any Communist-related cause could get one blacklisted. The only way to get off the blacklist was to provide the names of others who had been involved in such activities.

Congress revived the House Un-American Activities Committee (HUAC), which had been inactive during the war years, to investigate

Communist influence on the motion-picture industry. Screenwriters and actors were particular targets. Among the movies the committee denounced as Communist propaganda were such Oscar-winning films as *The Best Years of Our Lives* and *All the King's Men*, action movies like *The Adventures of Robin Hood*, and even schoolgirl romances like *Margie*. Ten Hollywood screenwriters were sentenced to prison for refusing to cooperate with the committee.

Motion-picture studio heads panicked. They produced a series of anti-Communist films like *I Married a Communist* and *I Was a Communist for the FBI*. In *My Son John*, a patriotic mother turns in her Communist son to the FBI, shouting "Take him away! He has to be punished!"[1]

HUAC also distributed a pamphlet called *One Hundred Things You Should Know About Communism*. It consisted of one hundred questions and answers. Question number seventy-six asked, "Where can a Communist be found in everyday life?" The answer: "Look for him in your school, your labor union, your church, or your civic club. (Really, everywhere.)"[2]

McCARTHYISM

By now the United States was fighting communism in Korea, and American boys were dying. It was unpatriotic to be anything but anti-Communist. The problem was that aggressive anti-Communists accused many innocent people. The fever of McCarthyism was spreading across the nation.

Joseph R. McCarthy was a Republican senator from Wisconsin. When China fell to the Communists in 1949, there had been accusations from his party that Communists in the State Department were responsible for allowing it to happen. In 1950, McCarthy made a speech to a Republican women's club, during which he waved some papers and announced that "I have here in my hand a list of 205 . . . members of the Communist Party . . . still working and shaping policy in the State Department."[3] Nobody ever actually saw the list.

By 1953, McCarthy was going full steam. When former president Harry Truman warned Americans against "the onslaught of fear and hysteria, which are being manipulated in this country purely for political purposes," McCarthy went on television to reply. The Truman administration had "crawled with Communists," he said, and then he accused ex-president Truman himself of aiding Communists.[4]

The following year McCarthy accused Secretary of the Army Robert T. Stevens of "concealing foreign espionage activities." The secretary responded that McCarthy had made threats against army officials in an effort to keep his assistant from being drafted into the military. During the Senate hearings that followed, Secretary Stevens was represented by attorney Joseph Nye Welch. When McCarthy made a particularly vicious charge against an associate of the lawyer, Welch responded: "Until this moment, Senator, I think I never gauged your cruelty, or your recklessness. Have you no sense of decency, sir? At long last, have you no sense of decency?"[5]

Welch's disgust heralded the end of McCarthyism. In December 1954 the Senate voted to condemn McCarthy for "conduct unbecoming a senator."[6] However, even though the country was disgusted by the excesses of McCarthyism, anticommunism would continue to ebb and flow in response to world events.

COMMIE PROTEST OR LEGITIMATE DISSENT?

A revolution in Cuba, only ninety-odd miles away from the United States off the coast of Florida, left a pro-Communist government in power in 1959. The Soviet Union rushed to support it with technical help and arms. When the Soviets began to build offensive missile bases in Cuba, America was pushed to the brink of war. A last-minute agreement between President John F. Kennedy and Soviet Premier Nikita Khrushchev in 1962 to remove the missiles and dismantle the missile launchers prevented the outbreak of hostilities. Nevertheless, the Cuban missile crisis, as it was called, stirred up fear of Soviet aggression and revived government anti-Communist efforts.

More stringent measures went into effect in the 1960s when the United States became involved in the Vietnam War. Once again, as in Korea, American boys were literally dying to keep the Communist half of a divided nation from taking over the non-Communist half. Nevertheless, there were mass protests at home against U.S. involvement. As the protests spread across the nation, the FBI, CIA, and other government organizations responded. They compiled secret dossiers on protest leaders and wiretapped peace groups. Police, using tear gas and billy clubs, brutally broke up anti-war demonstrations. When young college protestors were killed at Kent State University in Ohio and Jackson State College in Mississippi, public sentiment began to build against the government crackdown on protestors. Most Americans were still anti-Communist, but there was a feeling that the U.S. government was going too far in suppressing legitimate dissent.

FIGHTING FIRE WITH FIRE

By the 1980s a balance seemed to have been reached between legitimate anticommunism and the hysteria of McCarthyism. Although President Ronald Reagan called the USSR "the focus of evil in the modern world," he also met with Soviet Premier Mikhail Gorbachev. By December 1987 the two leaders had hammered out a weapons treaty between their two countries. In its aftermath, anticommunist sentiment in America began to diminish.

As a policy, American anticommunism had always been driven by the terrible things done in the Soviet Union and elsewhere in the name of communism. In reality, many of the techniques used by the Soviet Communists had also been used to some degree by authorities in the United States. The invasions of privacy, the threats and bullying, the loss of jobs and blacklisting, the clubs and the tear gas, and the shooting of protestors were all in the tradition of Soviet communism, not American democracy. It must be forcefully noted, however, that nothing that happened in the United States in the name of anticommunism remotely approached the extent or the horror of the Soviet Union's purges and persecution of its own citizens.

One of the evils of communism was that it too often pushed Americans into fighting fire with fire. But the fire in America was a flickering flame that died out. The fire in the Soviet Union was an inferno that consumed the nation. Hopefully, neither will ever flare up again.

CHAPTER
ONE

THE OPENING
ROUND

On 9 February 1946 Stalin made his "Two Camps" speech, in which he declared that communism and capitalism belonged to two different camps, fundamentally incompatible, and irreconcilable, and that peace was impossible until capitalism was vanquished and replaced by communism.

The speech that kicked off the Cold War

The extent of the damage suffered by the Soviet Union in World War II cannot be overstated. Eleven million Soviet soldiers were killed. An estimated 30 million were wounded, many of them crippled or otherwise incapacitated for life. Some 20 to 25 million Soviet civilians died prematurely as a result of the war. The Nazi armies had destroyed much of the food supply of the nation, as well as the railroads used to bring food to the people. In 1945 and early 1946, peace brought suffering and starvation to much of the Soviet population.

Premier Joseph Stalin chose to address a different problem. Factories, power plants, bridges, mines, and refineries had been destroyed during the war. Now they must be rebuilt. Stalin "demanded greatly increased productivity with the emphasis on heavy industry and armaments." There would be little manufacture of consumer goods. Much of the housing destroyed in the war would not be rebuilt. Food would continue to be scarce. We must, declared the sixty-six-year-old dictator, "raise our industry to a level, say three times as high as that of pre-war industry. We must see to it that our industry shall be able to produce annually up to 50 million tons of pig iron, up to 60 million tons of steel, up to 500 million tons of coal, and up to 60 million tons of oil. Only when we succeed in doing that can we be sure that our fatherland will be insured against all contingencies."[1] By "contingencies," he meant the threat of war with the United States.

THE IRON CURTAIN SPEECH

It has been suggested that in addition to being power-mad, Stalin became paranoid. "For twenty-seven years," his daughter, Svetlana, wrote, "I was witness to the spiritual deterioration of my own father, watching day after day how everything human in him left him and how gradually he turned into a grim monument to his own self."[2] Stalin's paranoia in regard to the United States was fueled by the knowledge that it had the atomic bomb, and the Soviets, as yet, did not. He had convinced himself that the United States intended to wage war on the USSR. A team of Soviet and captive German scientists was feverishly at work "under orders to catch up with the Americans as quickly as possible."[3] The project was supervised by the chief of the secret police, Lavrenti Beria.

World War II had ended with the knowledge that there were now two superpowers—the United States and the Soviet Union—and that they had very different world views. The United States was a democracy with a free-market system. The USSR was a dictatorship with a state-controlled economy. It had occupation forces throughout Eastern Europe, including Poland, Hungary, Romania, Bulgaria, East Germany, and parts of Austria and Finland. During the postwar 1940s, it would install puppet governments in those nations. These would create a buffer zone between the Soviet Union and the democracies of Western Europe.

On March 5, 1946, in Fulton, Missouri, former British prime minister Winston Churchill delivered what would come to be known as his Iron Curtain speech. "From Stettin in the Baltic to Trieste in the Adriatic," he declared, "an iron curtain has descended across the Continent. Behind that line lie all the capitals of the States of Central and Eastern Europe—Warsaw, Berlin, Prague, Vienna, Budapest, Belgrade, Bucharest, and Sofia. All these famous cities and the populations around them lie in the Soviet sphere, and all are subject in one form or another, not only to Soviet influence, but to a very high and increasing measure of control from Moscow."[4]

Stalin was furious. He called the address "a dangerous act." He condemned Churchill as "the warmonger of the Third World War," and compared him with Hitler. Efforts were stepped up to develop a Soviet atomic bomb.[5]

OIL! OIL! OIL!

The USSR had been America's ally during World War II, but when it was learned on February 3, 1946, that "a Soviet spy ring had successfully transmitted secret information about the U.S. atomic bomb to the Soviet Union," the government and the people of the United States were outraged and alarmed.[6] Their fear and suspicion increased when a Soviet plot to seize Iranian oil fields was revealed.

During World War II, American, British, and Soviet troops had all occupied parts of Iran. Because of its oil, and its strategically vital access to the Persian Gulf, securing Iran from the Germans had been important. At the wartime Yalta Conference, attended by U.S. President Franklin Roosevelt, British Prime Minister Winston Churchill, and Premier Joseph Stalin, the Soviet leader had promised that Soviet troops would withdraw from Iran "within six months after the war ended." Instead, in 1946 the Soviets tried to create an "autonomous region" of Iran to be annexed to the Soviet Socialist Republic of Azerbaijan.[7]

This was unacceptable to the United States. President Truman (who had taken over after Roosevelt's death in 1945) threatened to send troops to evict the Soviets from Iran. However, Stalin blinked, and the Red Army (as the Soviet military was known) withdrew from Iran in April 1946. At the same time, Stalin backed away from another showdown with the United States when it refused to allow the USSR to share control of the Dardanelles Straits with Turkey. At issue was oil and its free passage through the waterways of the world. For Iran's oil to fall into Soviet hands, wrote Truman, "would be a serious loss for the economy of the Western world." Also at risk were the Saudi Arabia oil reserves, "a stupendous source of strategic power, and one of the greatest material prizes in world history."[8]

CHINA: SOVIET ALLY OR RIVAL?

The opening of the Cold War did not just occur in the Middle East and Europe. It was a worldwide war between democracy and communism, between free markets and state ownership. Inevitably, it was a struggle that involved China, the most populous nation in the world, as well as other countries in Southeast Asia, notably Vietnam and Korea.

Korea had been occupied by the Japanese since 1910. Shortly before the World War II surrender by Japan, Soviet troops had occupied the northern part of Korea. After the Japanese surrender, on September 8, 1945, American troops landed in the southern part of Korea. It was agreed that the 38th parallel (of latitude) should be the dividing line between the Soviet occupation and the U.S. occupation. Both the Soviets and the Americans said that once the country was stabilized, power would be returned to the Koreans.

Stalin established control over the North Korean government and economy, ensuring that it would be both Communist and loyal to the Soviet Union. In China the situation was more complicated. At the end of World War II, Stalin had signed a treaty of friendship with Chiang Kai-shek, the leader of the anti-Communist Chinese Nationalist forces. On August 19, 1946, Chinese Communist leader Mao Tse-tung declared all-out war on those forces. The Communists eventually defeated Chiang and took over the whole of China. The establishment of a People's Republic of China, rather than a group of Chinese Soviet Socialist Republics ruled from Moscow, was a challenge to Stalin's power. China may have gone Communist, but from the Soviet view it was the wild card in the Cold War.

THE MARSHALL PLAN

If both the United States and the USSR were caught off balance by events in China, it was because they were focused on Europe. In the late 1940s they were also not paying much attention to events in the French colony of Vietnam. Here, in December 1946, forces of the Vietnamese Democratic Republic, led by Moscow-trained Communist President Ho Chi Minh, were waging a fierce war against the French rulers of Vietnam. Facing a well-armed, well-trained French colonial army, Ho had exhorted the Vietnamese people to "arm yourselves with axes and sticks."[9] It was a guerilla war against a colonial power that would evolve into a struggle that would one day involve the United States, the Soviet Union, and China.

Germany, not Vietnam, was the focal point during the early days of the Cold War. In May 1947 war-ravaged West Germany faced massive food shortages and the possibility of famine. The United States responded by rushing 1.2 million tons of food to the area. In June, U.S. Secretary of State George C. Marshall put forth the idea of a reconstruction plan for the countries of Europe devastated during World War II. Passed by Congress in 1948, this massive aid program became known as the Marshall Plan.

Stalin's reaction to the Marshall Plan was described by Vladimir Yerofeyev of the Soviet Foreign Ministry: "Stalin, with his suspicious nature, didn't like it. 'This is a ploy by Truman [Stalin said] . . . What they want is to infiltrate European countries.' . . . Stalin became even more suspicious and moved to stop the countries friendly to us taking part. Yugoslavia and Poland agreed. Finland too. . . . Nine countries refused to take part. . . ."[10]

THE BERLIN AIRLIFT

In March 1948 tensions between the United States and the Soviet Union came to a head in Berlin. The former capital city of Germany lay 125 miles inside Soviet-controlled East Germany. Nevertheless, the city had been split up into zones with West Berlin controlled by the Allies—the United States, Britain, and France—and East Berlin controlled by the Soviets. The general council that governed Berlin included both Allies and Soviets. When the council refused to form a central German government, and would not allow the USSR to share in German iron-ore production, the Soviets stormed out of the meeting. They then moved additional troops to the border between their zone in Berlin and the American zone.

A month later the Soviets began blocking all train, truck, and barge traffic from entering Berlin. Soon no food could be delivered. The city faced starvation. The Allies responded with the Berlin airlift, a massive effort to deliver food and other supplies to the city by air. The Soviets then

A group of Berliners anxiously awaits the landing of a U.S. Air Force plane bringing much-needed supplies to that blockaded city, where Soviets had shut down access to food and power from April 1948 until May 1949.

reduced coal shipments to the city and cut down on the electricity for the Allied sector. They seized six river barges loaded with food bound for Berlin from Hamburg.

The Berlin Airlift started out delivering six tons of food to the city every day, and worked up to 2,500 tons daily. The Allies spent $200 million to keep their planes flying in every kind of weather. The Berlin airlift stopped when the Soviets ended the blockade in May 1949, following negotiations with the United States under the sponsorship of the United Nations.

SATELLITE COUPS

Berlin was not the only place where the Soviets flexed their muscles in Europe. A coup sponsored by the Soviets and aided by Red Army officials resulted in the overthrow of Hungarian Premier Ferenc Nagy and the installation of a pro-Soviet government in Hungary. Soviet-backed Communists forced the abdication of King Michael of Romania and Romanian Communists tightened their hold on the government. In Czechoslovakia, where a coalition government had been formed between Communists and Democrats, another Soviet-backed coup took place.

When moderate members of the Czech cabinet resigned to protest Communist control over the police, Communist Prime Minister Klement Gottwald began to purge non-Communists from the government. Non-Communist political parties were outlawed. Gottwald pressured the democratically elected President Eduard Benes to form a "government of the workers."[11] While Benes considered resigning, popular democratic leader Jan Masaryk, son of the first president of the Czechoslovak Republic, decided to stay on as foreign minister.

At 6:00 A.M. on March 10, 1948, the lifeless body of Jan Masaryk was found three floors below an open window at the Foreign Ministry. The Gottwald government announced that he had committed suicide. Non-Communist Czechs accused the regime of murdering him to rid itself of a powerful democratic voice within the government. Three months later Benes finally resigned from the Communist government. Pro-Soviet Czech Communists were now in total control of Czechoslovakia.

[22]

Stalin was remarkably successful in establishing Soviet power over satellite countries. The exception was Yugoslavia. Here he met his match in Marshal Tito (Josip Broz), the Communist leader of the country, who had led the partisan fight against the Germans during World War II. The first meeting between them took place during the war in July 1944. At it, Stalin informed Tito that when the conflict ended, King Peter of Yugoslavia would have to be reinstated. Tito "told him it was impossible, that the people would rebel, that in Yugoslavia the king personified treason."[12]

Stalin was not used to being contradicted. He regarded Tito as a provincial Balkan peasant lacking the experience or ability to set up a Yugoslav government. He was silent for a long moment, and then he told Tito that "you need not restore him forever. Take him back temporarily and then you can slip a knife into his back at a suitable moment."[13]

Tito did not follow Stalin's advice. After the war, Tito successfully established his own Communist government in Yugoslavia. Before long, however, he was being charged by the Soviets with deviating from the Communist line. It was said that Tito was secretly cooperating with western imperialists. Tito struck back, charging that Soviet agents were trying to topple his government. In July 1948, when Tito made his independence clear, it constituted a final break with Moscow. Stalin no longer had control over *all* of the Communist regimes in Europe.

At that time, Stalin was preoccupied with developing a Soviet atomic bomb. In September 1949 his goal was realized. The Soviets successfully detonated a nuclear bomb. The Cold War would now be ruled by deterrence, meaning that each side would stockpile so many nuclear weapons that the other side would not dare use theirs. It would be a policy of challenges and standoffs, a game of chicken, but oddly enough, it would work.

THE LAST DAYS OF STALIN

> For the sake of its prestige, the USA might become involved in a big war; China will be drawn in and with it the USSR, which is tied by a pact of mutual assistance with China. . . . If war is inevitable, then let it happen now. . . .
>
> October 1950 letter from Stalin to Chinese Premier Mao Tse-tung following U.S. landings at Inchon during the Korean War

On March 5, 1949, Premier Kim Il-Sung of North Korea went to Moscow to meet Joseph Stalin. He asked for help from the Soviet Union to rebuild the Korean economy. Stalin agreed to provide $40 million plus Soviet specialists to help build new factories and plants. "We'll give you help in all military questions," Stalin promised, adding that "Korea must have military aircraft." Later that year, when North Korea crossed the border to probe the defenses of South Korea, Stalin was kept informed. According to Dmitri Volkogonov, former Soviet Union director of the Institute of Military History, "throughout 1949, the Soviet Union delivered weapons and other military equipment to North Korea at an intense pace, each consignment personally approved by Stalin."[1]

On January 19, 1950, Terenti Shtykov, the Soviet ambassador to North Korea, reported that "Kim Il-Sung needs to see Stalin to ask for permission to invade the South in order to liberate it. Kim Il-Sung said that he could not begin an offensive himself because he is a Communist, a man of discipline, and Comrade Stalin's instructions are for him the law."[2] Five months later Kim Il-Sung ordered North Korean troops to attack South Korea. It was the start of the Korean War.

Like Stalin, Korean leader Kim Il-Sung was the center of a cult of personality, a heroic figure whose life was made up of deeds and accomplishments blown up into lies and legends. He was a patriotic Korean, a loyal Communist, and the absolute ruler of his country for forty-six years. That made him the longest serving Communist leader in history. He was also the first Communist leader to establish a dynasty, a reign in which his son succeeded him.

In 1912, when Kim Il-Sung was born, Korea was a colony of Japan. The Japanese rule over Korea was extremely harsh. Korean culture and language were regarded as inferior. Japanese was the official language of Korea; schoolbooks were in Japanese, and classes were taught in Japanese. Young Kim rebelled against this. Using a penknife, he scratched out the title of the Japanese schoolbook he was required to read. "Whenever I saw children trying to learn Japanese," said Kim of his childhood years, "I told them Koreans must speak Korean."[3]

Around 1925, Kim's family fled to Manchuria in China to escape Japanese oppression. In 1929, Kim was expelled from school and briefly jailed for opposing Japanese colonial expansion into Manchuria. Upon his release, he joined an anti-Japanese guerilla group. When he was nineteen years old, he joined the illegal Chinese Communist Youth League.

Kim became the leader of a small band of Korean partisans within the Chinese Communist guerilla army in Manchuria. Throughout the 1930s, he led attacks on Japanese outposts across the Korean border. By 1940, however, the Japanese had cracked down on Kim's operations, and dispersed his Korean fighters. To avoid capture, Kim was forced to flee deep into eastern Siberia in the Soviet Union.

The Soviets were providing military training to guerillas. World War II was going on and Kim's training by the Soviets eventually led to his becoming a major in the Red Army. When Soviet forces drove the Japanese out of North Korea in August 1945, Kim was assigned by the Soviets to form and head up a provisional government. The Soviets provided support for Kim to organize a Korean People's Army. By 1947 a permanent North Korean government had been organized with Kim Il-Sung as its leader.

THE KOREAN WAR

In 1948 the United Nations (UN) appointed a commission to supervise elections that would determine the government of a unified Korea, which would include both the North and South. Kim Il-Sung refused to cooperate. On May 10 the elections were held in South Korea, and on July 17 the Republic of South Korea was established. In August the Democratic People's Republic of Korea was proclaimed in the north. It claimed authority over all of Korea. Kim "began advocating the violent overthrow of the South Korean government." He "ordered his Soviet-equipped armed forces to cross the 38th parallel into South Korea on 25 June 1950."[4]

Within three days, North Korean forces captured the South Korean capital city of Seoul. United States President Harry Truman, without asking Congress for a declaration of war, ordered that American troops stationed in Japan be flown to Korea to help the South Koreans fight off the invasion. His claim that he had the constitutional authority to involve the United States in a limited "police action" was disputed by his political opponents.[5] However, an emergency session of the United Nations Security Council, boycotted by the Soviet Union, approved military action by UN forces under American command.

Stalin was assured of victory by the North Koreans. Nevertheless, on June 30, he received an urgent request for additional military supplies including "fifteen million rifle bullets, 21.5 million pistol rounds, forty-three thousand revolver rounds, anti-aircraft guns and shells of various caliber, mortars, tank ammunition and hand grenades."[6] Stalin approved the list, and the munitions were sent.

CHINESE TROOPS ATTACK

On September 15 a massive UN force under the command of U.S. General Douglas MacArthur landed at Inchon and began to push the North Korean forces back beyond the 38th parallel and toward the Chinese border. On October 1, Kim Il-Sung notified Stalin of an "urgent need of direct military help from the Soviet Union." He added that "if for any reason this is not possible, then help us in establishing international volunteer units in China . . . to give us military assistance in our struggle."[7]

Stalin passed on the request to Chinese leaders Mao Tse-tung and Chou En-lai. The Chinese responded positively. On October 25, twelve Chinese divisions crossed into Korea to support a massive counteroffensive against UN (mostly American) troops. Twelve more divisions in China were being held in reserve to support them. On November 14, Stalin ordered the Soviet 64th Fighter Air Corps to provide cover for Chinese and North Korean ground troops. Over the three years of the Korean War, fifteen Soviet air divisions and several antiaircraft divisions saw action in Korea.

The combined Communist forces recaptured North Korea, while the UN and South Korean armies held onto South Korea. By early 1953, a stalemate had developed along the 38th parallel. On July 27, 1953, a cease-fire agreement was signed between the Communist forces and the UN forces. It called for a 155-mile-long Demilitarized Zone (DMZ) as the boundary between North Korea and South Korea. The Korean War was over. The Communists had not attained their objective. Korea was not reunified under Communist rule.

STALIN AND THE JEWS

During the Korean War, Stalin had become increasingly obsessed with the Jews of the Soviet Union. Prior to that, he had pretty much confined his anti-Semitism (hatred of Jews) to his personal relationships. When his son, Yakov, married a Jewish woman, Stalin had been furious. When Yakov was captured during World War II and the Germans offered to arrange a prisoner exchange, Stalin refused, calling his son a traitor because "no true Russian would ever surrender."[8] He had Yakov's Jewish wife imprisoned during the war. Later, when Stalin's daughter, Svetlana, fell in love with a Jew, he saw to it that the man spent ten years in prison camps where Svetlana could not contact him. When Svetlana subsequently married another Jew, Stalin forbid her to bring him home, shouting that her husband "was thrown your way by the Zionists."[9]

The Zionists, Jews who had fought to establish the state of Israel, were proclaimed the archenemy of communism by Stalin in the 1950s. It had not always been the case. In May 1947 the Soviet Union had cast its UN vote in support of the creation of the Jewish State of Israel. A year later when Israel became a nation, Stalin was the first to recognize its government.

There were two reasons for his initial support. He believed that Israel would be a Socialist state and that he could therefore bring it into the Soviet sphere of influence, an ambition which never came close to being accomplished. He also thought, correctly, that if Israel became a nation that would speed up the decline of British influence in the Middle East.

Stalin's positive policy toward Jews actually began during World War II. In March 1942 he had established the Jewish Anti-Fascist Committee "to raise funds for the Soviet war effort" among Jews abroad. Because of Hitler's campaign against the Jews, and because the Soviets were locked in battle with the Nazis, their efforts "proved a phenomenal success," particularly in America.[10]

THE SURGE OF ANTI-SEMITISM

Members of the Soviet Jewish Anti-Fascist Committee were pro-Zionist, and in the 1950s, reacting to strong U.S. support for Israel, Stalin proclaimed Zionism unpatriotic. British historian Sir Alan Bullock writes that "Stalin succumbed to the same virus of anti-Semitism as Hitler."[11] Jews who were loyal Soviet Communists were classified as Zionist spies and traitors by Stalin. The members of the Jewish Anti-Fascist Committee were arrested and subjected to around-the-clock interrogation, torture, and anti-Semitic abuse. The official in charge of them wrote to Stalin that "I especially hated and was pitiless toward Jewish nationalists, whom I saw as the most dangerous and evil enemies."[12]

During the four years they were in prison, some of the committee succumbed and confessed to treasonous activities. However, they later recanted and said they had been forced to confess. This sequence was repeated several times. Finally six of them were worn down, again confessed, and were brought to trial along with nine others whom they had supposedly implicated. When they were brought into the courtroom, however, four of the six flatly repudiated their confessions. All fifteen were tried anyway.

Three military judges presided. There was no jury. There were no prosecutors or defense attorneys. Spectators and press were barred from the courtroom. In the summer of 1952, thirteen of the fifteen Jews were found guilty and executed.

THE DOCTORS' PLOT

During the trial, Stalin, now in his seventies, was not feeling well. His personal physician, Dr. Vladimir N. Vinogradov, the president of the Moscow Medical Society, examined him. Dr. Vinogradov found that Stalin was suffering from "hypertension and arteriosclerosis." He recommended that Stalin "retire from all public activity." Stalin flew into a rage, shouting, "Throw him in chains!" at the doctor. By November 1952, Dr. Vinogradov was indeed in shackles, one of the few non-Jews accused in the so-called Doctors' Plot.[13]

The Doctors' Plot began with Lydia Timashuk. She was a radiologist who had attracted Stalin's attention back in 1939 when she proposed a contest to find ways to prolong the life of Comrade Stalin. Now an informant for the secret police, she bypassed her superiors, including secret police chief Lavrenti Beria, and wrote directly to Stalin that she had uncovered a plot by Dr. Vinogradov and seven other renowned Soviet physicians "to cut short the lives of active public figures of the Soviet Union through sabotage medical treatment."[14]

The doctors were alleged to have killed two former members of the elite panel appointed by the Central Committee of the Communist party, known as the Politburo, and to have "sought to put out of action several chiefs of the armed forces."[15] They were accused of working for American and British intelligence. Seven of the accused doctors were Jews. After they were taken into custody, there was a rash of arrests of Jewish officials in the public health, economic, and foreign ministries, as well as in the universities of Moscow. The Jewish head of the news agency *Tass* was arrested. General L. Z. Mekhlis, the chief political commissar of the Red Army, who happened to be a Jew, tried to flee. He was caught and shot. The Soviet Union broke off diplomatic relations with Israel.

THE DEATH WATCH

Prosecution of those involved in the Doctors' Plot, was put on hold in early March 1953 when Stalin suffered a cerebral hemorrhage. The official radio announcement said that "the best medical brains have been summoned to

Comrade Stalin's treatment."[16] According to the announcement, he had been stricken in his Moscow apartment.

A different version held that Stalin had received various Soviet officials in his office in the Kremlin (the Soviet capital building) and that they had attacked his proposal to deport all Soviet Jews. Stalin, according to this account, went into a rage and ordered Beria to arrest "all the scum here."[17] When Beria refused, Stalin sprang up, screamed, lost consciousness, and fell. A variation of this story is that he struck his head and was given a glass of brandy. The brandy was allegedly poisoned.

A more believable report comes from Nikita Khrushchev, a future premier of the Soviet Union. According to him, on the evening of February 28, Stalin drank too much at dinner and did not go to bed until early on the morning of March 1. Neither Khrushchev nor Stalin's daughter was able to reach him that day. The next morning a doctor was summoned and it was determined that Stalin had suffered a stroke.

Among other high-ranking Soviet officials, Khrushchev and Beria spent several hours in the sickroom. According to Khrushchev, while Stalin lay in a coma, Beria mocked and insulted him. However, when Stalin temporarily regained consciousness and it appeared that he might recover, Beria dropped to his knees, took Stalin's hand, and proclaimed his loyalty.

Stalin's condition worsened. Leeches were applied to his neck and the back of his head to suck out any poison that might be in his system. It was to no avail. At 9:50 P.M. on March 5, Joseph Stalin died.

Beria was in charge of the security arrangements for the funeral. His men, wearing blue-and-white caps, sealed off streets and regulated access to Moscow's Red Square, where the final ceremonies were to take place. They herded the crowds of mourners brutally, as if they were stampeding cattle. Historian H. Montgomery Hyde describes how "several hundreds of people were trampled underfoot and crushed to death between the traffic lights and the trucks of Beria's security guards," adding that "it was as if Stalin had claimed his last victims from the grave."[18]

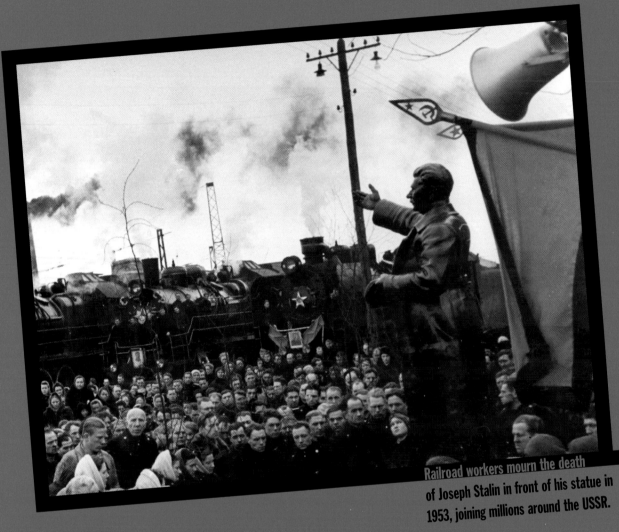

Railroad workers mourn the death of Joseph Stalin in front of his statue in 1953, joining millions around the USSR.

BERIA AND MALENKOV

> # When I die, the imperialists will strangle all of you like a litter of kittens.
>
> Joseph Stalin to his closest subordinates
> three months before his death

The "litter" included Lavrenti Beria, Georgi Malenkov, Vyachaslav Molotov, Nikolai Bulganin, and Nikita Khrushchev. Immediately after Stalin's death, the most powerful among them was Lavrenti Beria. Before the year was over, Beria would be executed.

Beria had become the head of the NKVD, the Soviet secret police, in 1938. He had been responsible for reorganizing the gulags (Soviet labor camps), and for the brutal treatment of the political prisoners that populated them. During World War II he had been in charge of the Katyn Forest massacre, in which some 15,000 Polish prisoners of war had died. At the end of the war Beria had overseen the mass exiles and killings of Ukrainians, Chechens, and others suspected of collaborating with the Germans. In 1946, when the NKVD was reorganized into the MVD (Ministry of the Interior) and MGB (Political Police), the Beria lackey who now headed the secret police reported directly to Beria before being seen by Stalin. Beria remained in charge of the army of men who made up the MVD and the MGB.

Immediately after Stalin's death, Beria's forces sealed off Moscow with tanks and flamethrowers. The commander of the Moscow Military District, the officers of the city's army garrison, and the Kremlin guards were all put under arrest. Various high government officials were removed from positions of power. Georgi Malenkov, a Stalin loyalist, became prime minister of the USSR and first secretary of the Communist party. He was selected because Beria was sure he could control him. Beria was named one of Malenkov's four first deputy prime ministers. There were rumors in Moscow, and later throughout the Soviet Union, "that Stalin was murdered and that Malenkov and Beria . . . had a hand in it."[1]

MALENKOV'S CHOICE

Georgi Malenkov was born on January 8, 1902, in Orenburg, Russia. He joined the Bolshevik—later the Communist—party in 1920. Rising through the ranks, he was active in promoting the Stalinist purges of the 1930s. In World War II, he was one of Stalin's most trusted subordinates. He was named a full member of the Politburo in 1946. During the period just before Stalin's death, it was well known that Stalin was grooming Malenkov to succeed him.

Beria had forcefully backed Malenkov. He had great insight into the character of Malenkov. There were similarities between the two men, but there were also differences. Both had known how to curry favor with Stalin. Both had a talent for fawning and manipulating. Both had recognized Stalin as the center of power, and both had siphoned off some of that power for themselves while increasing it for Stalin.

Both were unscrupulous, but Beria was hard and unyielding while Malenkov knew how to compromise when it was to his advantage. Malenkov would go along to get along. He did what he had to do to ensure Beria's support. Beria saw Malenkov as weak and malleable, and thought that he would have no trouble controlling Malenkov. However, Beria miscalculated.

Malenkov was weak, but he was astute when it came to Soviet politics. He saw that there was a choice to be made between being Beria's puppet and compromising with those who wanted to share the power of government. Beria had many enemies. They were powerful and dangerous, and Malenkov did not want them to be his enemies as well. He recognized that those who had been forced out of government could not be restrained permanently. If he did not deal with them, he would always have to be watch-

Georgi Malenkov replaced Stalin as prime minister and leader of the Communist party. It was under his regime that the Soviet Union successfully exploded its own hydrogen bomb, firmly pitting the USSR against the United States.

ing his back. Despite Beria's show of force in his favor, Malenkov was not secure enough as a leader to get away with staging a Stalinist-type purge to rid himself of adversaries. It made more sense to negotiate with powerful rivals like Nikolai Bulganin and Nikita Khrushchev. Ten days after he assumed office, Malenkov double-crossed Beria.

BERIA: TWISTING IN THE WIND

Without warning, Malenkov announced that "because of his responsibilities as prime minister he wished to be relieved of his post as first secretary of the Communist party."[2] This cut him off from the party machine, which Stalin had used to enforce his decisions. When the post of first secretary of the Communist Party was not filled following Malenkov's resignation, Deputy First Minister Khrushchev took over the duties without being officially named to the post. He worked behind the scenes with the minister of state security to purge Beria's men from the MVD and the MGB.

Whatever their private opinions, none of those now in positions of power—Khrushchev, Malenkov, Beria, Molotov, and Bulganin—had spoken out against the prosecution of those involved in the Doctors' Plot. Nevertheless, less than a month after Stalin's death, the Doctors' Plot was being officially labeled a "provocation and fake."[3] A general amnesty was declared and tens of thousands of political prisoners, among them the accused doctors and many other Jews caught up in the Stalinist net, were set free.

Seeing which way the wind was blowing, Beria revealed that the Doctors' Plot had been a crude Stalinist frame-up. Never mentioning his own guilt, he loudly attacked the dead dictator. "Stalin was a scoundrel," he shouted, "a villain, a tyrant! He terrorized all of us, that blood-thirsty devil!"[4]

Repudiating Stalin did not save Lavrenti Beria. On June 26, 1953, he was arrested by his colleagues in the Kremlin. He was accused of being an enemy agent, and a "malignant enemy of the Soviet people."[5] He was confined in a military prison and interrogated for several months. In December this executioner of so many innocent people was himself executed.

REBELLION IN EAST BERLIN

Earlier in June, the month that Beria was arrested, workers in East Berlin rebelled. The capital city of Soviet-occupied East Germany had long been the center of confrontation with troops of the Western democracies in West Berlin since 1948. The people of East Berlin had only to look across the checkpoints to see how much better West Berliners lived. Their resentment reached the boiling point when the East German Communist government announced an increase in production quotas for construction workers. What this meant was longer hours and harder work with no increase in pay. The government also threatened layoffs of workers who could not keep up with the new demands.

In East Berlin five thousand workers left their jobs and gathered in the streets to protest. Other workers throughout East Germany joined, and soon there were 50,000 people rioting in the streets of East Berlin. The East German government tried to cancel the new work rules, but it was too late. The riots continued. Workers attacked the Soviet Embassy, sat in at government offices, burned Communist flags, destroyed boundary markers between East and West Berlin, and set a border post on fire. A high official was dragged from his government limousine and beaten up. Soon loud-speaker trucks were crisscrossing the city urging all workers and their families to join the strikers.

When police could not subdue the rioters, Malenkov ordered Soviet troops and tanks into East Berlin to restore order. The Red Army closed off the border between East and West Berlin. They shut down the major highway joining East and West Germany. Soviet tanks lined up across from West Berlin with their guns in firing position. Soviet soldiers forced protesters back into their homes. They later entered these homes and dragged out those suspected of involvement in the strike. Before it was over, twenty people had been killed and nearly two hundred injured. The Soviet military commander imposed a curfew, and declared that East Berlin was now under martial law.

The Soviets said they would not reopen the city until the Americans, British, and French "guarantee to cease sending provocateurs and other criminal elements" into East Berlin. Communist East German Premier Otto Grotewohl blamed the rebellion on "Fascist and other reactionary elements" infiltrated from West Berlin. He said they had been incited by "foreign powers."[6]

When an alleged rioter from West Berlin was executed by the Communists, the Allied powers protested. They denied having anything to do with the demonstrations. They strongly condemned the use of force by the Soviet Union in East Berlin.

THE H-BOMB THREAT

Creating a Soviet satellite out of East Germany had been intended to expand the reach of the Soviet Union and spread the doctrine of communism. East Germany was seen as a source of reparations for the damages the Nazi invasion had inflicted on the USSR. Now, eight years after the end of the war, it wasn't working out that way. The Soviet Union was providing far more help to rebuild the East German economy than it was receiving in reparations. The East Germans were proving reluctant Communists, jealous of the prosperity the Marshall Plan had brought to West Germany. There was a constant flow of East Berlin defectors seeking refuge in West Berlin.

The North Atlantic Treaty Organization (NATO) was pledged to defend both West Germany and West Berlin. At this time NATO was made up of fourteen anti-Communist nations led by the United States, and pledged to provide troops and arms in the event of Communist aggression. NATO had recently reached an accord on a "long-range arms plan, relying heavily on nuclear weapons."[7] Malenkov had to take the threat very seriously because the United States had successfully exploded the world's first hydrogen bomb at Eniwetok Atoll in the Pacific Ocean on November 6, 1952. Malenkov reacted to this by announcing in a nationwide radio address delivered on August 8, 1953, that "we consider that there is no objective grounds for a collision between the United States and the USSR."[8]

A few days later he changed his tune. He announced that the Soviet Union had exploded its own hydrogen bomb. Malenkov proudly declared "that the United States no longer has a monopoly on the production of the hydrogen bomb."[9] His message was clear. The stakes in the Cold War were being raised.

BUTTER, NOT GUNS

In September 1953, Malenkov's position was undermined when Nikita Khrushchev officially became first secretary of the Communist party of the Soviet Union. Beginning with Leningrad, his first act was to replace party officials in cities throughout the Soviet Union with his own appointees. They in turn appointed Khrushchev loyalists to intermediate posts of authority. Quietly, Khrushchev purged the party of Malenkov supporters. Slowly, the nationwide party apparatus came under his control.

Around this time, encouraged by the release of political prisoners and the arrest of Beria, independent voices had begun to be raised in the Soviet Union. One historian of the period describes it as "a queer situation" in which "philosophers, scientists of every kind, artists of every kind, were rising and being encouraged to rise, in revolt against the dead hand of [the] party." Malenkov understood the shift in public attitudes and went along with them. Now, "all those who were fighting for more freedom saw Malenkov as their hope."[10]

Malenkov also offered hope to the peasant farmers who made up the majority of the Soviet population. Without consulting any of the leaders of the Communist party, or its first secretary, Nikita Khrushchev, he broke with a twenty-five year Soviet policy of developing heavy industry while short-changing agricultural development and production of consumer goods. He proposed to "raise sharply in two or three years the population's supply of foodstuffs and manufactured goods, meat and meat produce, fish and fish products, butter, sugar, eggs, confectionery, textiles, clothes, footwear, crockery, furniture and other cultural and household goods."[11] This could only be done by cutting back on armaments production and military appropriations. Subsequently, Malenkov announced that production of food was on the rise and there was no threat of famine.

FOOD FOR THOUGHT

Khrushchev saw that Malenkov had overstepped himself. The entire Soviet establishment, and particularly the Communist party, which Khrushchev controlled, was committed to maintaining a large military

CHAPTER FOUR

KHRUSHCHEV AND BULGANIN

> About the capitalist states, it doesn't depend on you whether or not we exist. If you don't like us, don't accept our invitation, and don't invite us to come and see you. Whether you like it or not, history is on our side. We will bury you.
>
> Nikita Khrushchev

Nikolai Bulganin and Nikita Khrushchev were born a year apart, Khrushchev in 1894 in Kalinovka, Russia, and Bulganin in 1895 in Gorky (then called Nizhni Novgorod), Russia. Bulganin came from a well-to-do family and received an excellent private-school education. Khrushchev was born into a poor peasant family; his father was a coal miner, and in his teens Khrushchev worked in the mines.

Khrushchev's peasant image stayed with him throughout his life. His broad features, snub nose, and large protruding ears conveyed the good-natured openness of the honest and simple "man of the earth" he declared himself to be.[1] Actually, Khrushchev was much more complicated. He had cultivated humor, energy, and a plainspoken manner to disguise the shrewdness, guile, and ruthlessness that marked his career.

His demeanor was shaggy, his clothes rumpled, his attitude that of the uneducated common man with little patience for intellectuals. Aside from his Communist politics, on a gut level he was contemptuous of the rich. When he met Nelson Rockefeller, an American whose name was synonymous with capitalist wealth, Khrushchev rudely poked him in the ribs and, with thinly disguised scorn, said, "So this is Mr. Rockefeller himself."[2]

If Khrushchev was often brusque and undiplomatic, Bulganin was the opposite. He was a charming man of quick wit and intelligence. He dealt smoothly with diplomats from the United States and the European countries. Always well tailored, he was a popular guest at embassy cocktail parties. Where Khrushchev was blunt and sometimes offensive, Bulganin was courteous and tactful.

The two met in Moscow in 1934 when Bulganin was Chairman of the Moscow City Soviet (sometimes called mayor of Moscow), and Khrushchev was supervising the construction of the city's subway system. They had arrived in Moscow by very different routes. Bulganin had joined the *Cheka*, as the Bolshevik secret police were then known, in 1917. His success in rooting out and executing anti-Bolsheviks earned him a position as an economic planner with the Supreme Economic Council. One reason for the appointment was that Bulganin had received a much better education than most of those in the Soviet bureaucracy, and was equipped to deal with complex problems. This led to his 1927 assignment as director of Electrovazod, the largest electrical equipment factory in the Soviet Union. His success in increasing the factory's production brought him to Stalin's attention, and resulted in his becoming chairman of the Moscow Soviet.

Bulganin had not fought in either the Russian Revolution or the civil war that followed it. Khrushchev, on the other hand, fought on the Bolshevik side in the civil war from 1918 through 1921. After leaving military service, Khrushchev took advantage of the adult school system set up by the Soviet regime. Here he received a basic education and was indoctrinated with Communist dogma. Khrushchev had joined the Communist party in the late spring of 1918. Now he was drawn into the circle of Stalin loyalists, and rose to a position of leadership.

In 1929, Khrushchev went to Moscow to study at the Academy of Heavy Industry. Here he became one of the top people in the Moscow Communist party and came to the attention of Stalin. In 1934, Khrushchev became a member of the Central Committee of the Soviet Communist party, which was made up of roughly a hundred leading Stalinists. Bulganin also joined the Central Committee.

THE VOICE OF THE PURGES

Between 1934 and 1938, most of the members of the Central Committee fell victim to the Stalinist purges and were executed. Bulganin, regarded as "a bright young Stalinist at a time when 'Old Bolsheviks' were arrested and killed by the tens of thousands," was not a victim.[3] Instead, as the purges opened up various high positions, he was promoted. He was made premier of the Russian Republic (the largest and most important of the Soviet states), and then advanced to deputy premier of the USSR and head of the state bank.

Meanwhile, Khrushchev played a more active role in the Stalinist purges. The victims of the purges were loyal Communists who had disagreed with one or another of Stalin's constantly shifting policies. Khrushchev called them "double dealers and murderers, agents of fascism," and urged using a "proletarian sword to chop off the heads of the loathsome creatures."[4]

In 1938, Khrushchev was sent to the Ukraine as first secretary of the Ukrainian Communist party. At this time some 150,000 Ukrainian party members had been arrested by the secret police. The executive Khrushchev replaced had been arrested, tortured, and killed. Under Khrushchev, the purges in the Ukraine tapered off and finally stopped. He successfully increased the region's agricultural production. During the conquest of Poland, which followed the 1939 Nazi-Soviet peace pact, Khrushchev was in charge of incorporating former Polish lands into the Soviet Ukraine.

TASTING, DANCING, AND ADVANCING

During World War II, Khrushchev served in the army, rising to the rank of lieutenant general. Bulganin was a member of the State Defense Committee during the war, and later was named first deputy minister of defense. In 1949, Stalin promoted him to vice-premier of the USSR. Stalin also brought Khrushchev to Moscow to serve as first secretary of the Moscow agricultural region.

Khrushchev became a top aide to Stalin. One of his duties was to taste the dictator's food to make sure it wasn't poisoned. Once Stalin ordered

Khrushchev, then in his mid-fifties, to perform the *gopak*. This is a traditional dance that calls for squatting down with folded arms and kicking to a fast beat. For Khrushchev, it was "sheer torture."[5]

After Stalin's death, Khrushchev and Bulganin became close allies. Bulganin was the more experienced one, the one who had risen highest in the Soviet government, the more popular one. It was relatively easy to arrange for Bulganin to replace Malenkov. Everyone in the Soviet hierarchy liked Bulganin. But it was understood that Khrushchev would be calling the shots.

CHINA AND YUGOSLAVIA

As first secretary of the Communist party, Nikita Khrushchev was concerned with non-Soviet Communist states, particularly China and Yugoslavia. In his last days, Stalin regarded Chinese Premier Mao Tse-tung as a rival leader of world communism rather than a Communist ally, and relations between China and the USSR were strained. In December 1954, as Malenkov was about to be toppled as premier, Khrushchev and Bulganin had gone to China to meet with Chairman Mao. Determined to improve the relationship between their two countries, Khrushchev had made territorial concessions involving disputed borderlands to China. He had also negotiated an agreement for the Soviet Union to supply China with the large amounts of raw materials and machinery needed to modernize its infrastructure. The visit was a major diplomatic success.

Efforts to patch things up with Communist Yugoslavia were not so effective. Ever since 1948, Yugoslavia's Marshal Tito had maintained his independence from Moscow. Now, on May 26, 1955, Khrushchev led a high-ranking delegation, including Premier Bulganin, to Yugoslavia's capital city of Belgrade to meet with Tito. Urging collaboration between their two countries in the interest of Communist solidarity against capitalism, Khrushchev blamed the trouble between them on lies circulated by the traitor Beria. It was an absurd excuse, and Tito angrily rejected it. Later in the visit, Khrushchev drank too much and passed out at an official reception. Tito helped carry him to his quarters.

Despite the bad start, Khrushchev's efforts did to some extent relax USSR tensions with Yugoslavia. The two countries resumed the diplomatic relations, which had ended during the Stalin era. However, Tito refused to reestablish a relationship between the Yugoslavian Communist party and the Soviet Communist party. He still did not want Yugoslavian Communist policy dictated by Moscow.

THE WARSAW PACT

Yugoslavia did not join the Warsaw Pact, the Communist military alliance formed on May 14, 1955. The Soviet Union had been the moving force behind the agreement, incited by the Allied nations admitting West Germany to NATO and granting its government authority to rearm. Those signing the Warsaw Pact included the USSR, Poland, Czechoslovakia, Hungary, Romania, Bulgaria, Albania, and East Germany. It established a total military strength of six million European Communist troops. The pact's most controversial provision provided for the maintenance of Soviet army units on the territories of all member nations. It has been described as a "systematic plan to strengthen the Soviet hold over its satellites."[6]

Europe was not the pair's only concern. Khrushchev regarded the Third World (so-called because its poor, industrially backward countries were not aligned with either the Communist or democratic blocs of nations) as fertile ground for alliances. He was well received on visits to Burma, Afghanistan, and India. In particular, he established a firm and long-lasting friendly relationship with India, home to the world's largest non-Communist population. Agreements with Egypt, which later led to Soviet help in building the Nile River's Aswan Dam, improved attitudes toward the Soviet Union throughout the Arab world.

At the same time, Khrushchev was flexing his nuclear muscles. On November 26, 1955, the USSR announced that it had exploded a "most powerful" hydrogen bomb. According to Khrushchev, the bomb "was equal to one million tons of TNT—a megaton." The Soviet Union admitted continuing to test "new types of atomic and thermonuclear weapons," claiming the tests were "in the interest of guaranteeing her security."[7]

KHRUSHCHEV DENOUNCES STALINISM

As the Cold War was picking up speed, there were changes in the Soviet Union. Tens of thousands of political prisoners had been released from gulag camps, and the relatives of hundreds of thousands more were demanding that they, too, must be pardoned. Releasing them, however, would imply that they had been wrongly punished. It would be an admission that the Stalinist purges had been unjust. It would be an accusation against those who had participated in them. These included Khrushchev himself. Like him, many of those involved in the purges still held high positions in the government.

Khrushchev met the problem head-on. On February 24, 1956, he went before the Twentieth Congress of the Soviet Communist party and put his control of that organization on the line. In a 26,000-word speech, he denounced Joseph Stalin. He charged him with being responsible for the execution of thousands of "honest Communists." He accused him of being behind the extortion of false confessions obtained by torture. He condemned Stalin's "megalomania," and his self-glorifying "cult of the individual," which had done great harm to the Soviet Union.[8]

Then Khrushchev denounced Stalin's foreign policies. "During Stalin's leadership," he said, "our peaceful relations with other nations were often threatened, because one-man decisions could cause, and often did cause, great complications." He quoted Stalin as having boasted that "I shall shake my little finger and there will be no more Tito," and of issuing threats of a "colonial nature" against China.[9]

In follow-up speeches, Khrushchev said that war between capitalism and communism was no longer inevitable. He spoke of "peaceful coexistence" with the United States.[10] However, in the United States, President Dwight D. Eisenhower's administration called the address "propagandistic." State Department officials pointed out that "state-sponsored murder, mass arrests and physical and mental torture continue to exist in the Soviet Union."[11]

Nikita Khrushchev denounces Stalin's domestic and foreign policies in a 1956 meeting of the Soviet Communist party in an attempt to distance himself from those abuses. However, Khrushchev's regime would turn out to be just as repressive.

POLISH WORKERS REVOLT

Such abuses would soon be seen in the Soviet satellite nations. Even as Khrushchev succeeded on June 2, 1956, in abolishing the USSR Justice Ministry, responsible for many of the horrors of the Stalinist purges, developments in Poland, and later in Hungary, would result in the Soviet army brutally trampling human rights. On June 28 workers in the Stalin Engineering Works in Posnan, Poland, went on strike. Strikes in Communist-ruled Poland were, of course, illegal. Nevertheless, the workers walked off their jobs, demanding higher pay. They were soon joined by other Posnan laborers chanting, "We want bread!"[12] Food shortages were severe in this city of 300,000 people, and living standards were low even compared to those in the Soviet Union.

Soon the demonstrations turned into riots. Red banners with Communist slogans were torn down and ripped to shreds. The strikers stormed the headquarters of the Polish United Workers, an anti-labor organization run by the Communist party.

Khrushchev's denunciation of Stalin incited the rioters' demands. Demonstrators insisted that the Polish Stalinists who were running the government be removed from office. Khrushchev reluctantly lent his support to a new government headed by the anti-Stalinist Wladislaw Gomulka. Immediate reforms were instituted by Gomulka. These went far beyond what Khrushchev had in mind, and he ordered the Polish leader to cancel some of them. Gomulka "refused to comply and instead threatened to call upon the Polish people to resist the Soviet pressure."[13] Khrushchev backed down.

THE HUNGARIAN REVOLUTION

Hungary was a different story. In July 1953 a new prime minister, Imre Nagy (no relation to former premier Ferenc Nagy), had come to power with a reform program. He legalized individual farm ownership and free trade. Internment camps where anti-Communists were held were abolished. The ban on travel was lifted. He announced that Hungary would have trade relations with capitalist as well as Communist countries. Because of his increased insistence on independence from the Soviet

Union, Nagy was forced out of office by Moscow-controlled Hungarian Communists in 1955.

In October 1956 student-led anti-Communist demonstrations broke out in Budapest, the capital city of Hungary. The protestors demanded the removal of Soviet troops from Hungarian soil, and the return to power of Imre Nagy. By October 23 the demonstrations had turned into an armed revolt.

When the demonstrators stormed the government's radio station, police fired on them. Rocks and bottles were hurled back. Students climbed a 23-foot statue of Stalin and chopped off its head. Government spokespersons denounced the protestors as "Fascist reactionary elements." A Hungarian Politburo member said the protestors were "trying to bring back capitalism. They must capitulate, or we will crush them." However, they neither capitulated nor were crushed. Instead, with hundreds of thousands of rebels still in the streets, their leaders met with government representatives and hammered out an agreement that returned Nagy to office.[14]

At the end of October, Nagy's government announced that Hungary would no longer be a one-party nation ruled by Communists, and would leave the Warsaw Pact. On the morning of November 4, the Soviets responded. Two hundred thousand Red Army troops and 5,500 tanks attacked Budapest. Russian planes roared over Hungary. Nagy ordered the Hungarian military to fight the Soviets, but their forces were too small in number, and the order came too late. By November 8 the Hungarian rebellion was crushed. Between 20,000 and 25,000 Hungarians had been killed, and some 200,000 had fled across the Austrian border before the Soviets sealed it.

A Moscow-controlled government took over in Hungary. Imre Nagy was arrested and later executed. Hungary would be a Soviet-dominated satellite for the next thirty-three years.

SPUTNIK!

In the Soviet Union, following the Hungarian revolution, there was opposition to Khrushchev's reorganization of the police and justice systems, and to the high-handed manner in which he made changes. Through his control of the Communist party, he had established a system of one-man rule that rendered Premier Bulganin a mere figurehead. A plot organized by Malenkov and other powerful government figures almost succeeded in removing Khrushchev from his position as first secretary of the Communist party. The coup was foiled with the help of Defense Minister Georgi Zhukov, the renowned World War II commander, who had troops and fleets of planes at his disposal. Zhukov rounded up the plotters. Malenkov was exiled to Siberia; some of the others to Outer Mongolia.

This all faded from the public consciousness in October 1957, when the Soviets launched *Sputnik*, the first man-made satellite, into orbit around the Earth. Weighing 184 pounds, six times as heavy as the satellite the United States was in the process of developing, *Sputnik* was a ball 23 inches in diameter. It circled the Earth once every ninety-five minutes. It broadcast continuous signals on two radio frequencies. The USSR and the United States had been rivals all through the 1950s in the race to conquer space. Now the Soviets had a decided lead.

On November 3 they launched a second satellite six times heavier than *Sputnik*. This one carried a dog named Laika, as well as a variety of measuring instruments. There was now an even greater gap in the space race. It was made more threatening by a Soviet prediction of a "launching of a satellite which will exist for tens and hundreds of years."[15] Such a device would be able to monitor U.S. defense preparations and military movements.

KHRUSHCHEV OVER ALL

Even as he was gloating over Soviet superiority in space, Khrushchev was making plans to get rid of Defense Minister Zhukov, the man who had saved him from a coup a few short months before. Khrushchev believed that Zhukov was creating a cult of personality with himself at the center. It was reported that "he had posed on a white stallion for a life-size portrait."[16] The memory of the Stalin cult of personality fresh in his mind, Khrushchev saw this as a giant step on the road to Zhukov's seizing power.

On November 3, 1957, Georgi Zhukov was removed from his post as defense minister. The Central Committee of the Khrushchev-controlled Soviet Communist party expelled Zhukov from the party. He was accused of having inflated his genuinely remarkable war record so that he would appear as a hero to the Soviet people. He was charged with having interfered with government control of the military and using it for his own purposes. (He had actually been helping Khrushchev at the time, but of course that wasn't mentioned.)

Nikolai Bulganin was now the only one between Khrushchev and control of the Soviet Union. However, Bulganin was a very weak obstacle indeed, and easily removed. On March 27, 1958, Bulganin resigned and Khrushchev replaced him as premier while holding onto his position as first secretary of the Communist party. In Khrushchev's subsequent speech to the more than 200 million citizens of the Soviet Union, he promised that "we shall conquer capitalism with a high level of work and a higher standard of living."[17] In the United States, Khrushchev's use of the word "conquer" was viewed as the latest missile hurled by the Soviets in the Cold War.

CHAPTER
FIVE

STEPS TO
A WALL

> Sixteen years have passed since World War Two. The USSR lost twenty million people in that war, and many of its areas were devastated. Now Germany, the country which unleashed World War II, has again acquired military power and has assumed a dominant position in NATO.
>
> Khrushchev defines the threat of a third world war to President Kennedy

In the summer of 1958, Nikita Khrushchev went to Peking, China, to meet with Chairman Mao Tse-tung, the head of the Chinese Communist government. One of Khrushchev's goals was to establish that with Bulganin out of the picture, he was now the sole leader not only of the Soviet Union, but of world communism as well. His claim went unchallenged at this meeting, but later that would change.

Khrushchev and Mao discussed military cooperation between their two countries. They agreed that the greatest threat to world peace came from Western "imperialist war maniacs."[1] Mao reassured Khrushchev that "in case of war, the Soviet Union may use any part of China; Russian sailors may come into any port in China." Khrushchev told him that "with our intercontinental missiles we have the Americans by the throat."[2]

THE BAY OF PIGS

A few months later Khrushchev's boast was made more ominous by the start of a chain of events that would create a Soviet ally out of the island nation of Cuba, 90 miles off the coast of Florida. A poor nation whose people lived in poverty, Cuba had long been exploited by American syndicates (organizations involved in the sugar and gambling businesses, for example) with the cooperation of its dictator, Fulgencio Batista. On New Year's Eve, 1958, rebel troops commanded by Fidel Castro seized the capital city of Havana and drove Batista's government from the country. Soon afterward, Castro confiscated all American-owned property in Cuba.

U.S.-owned sugar plantations and sugar mills were seized. Sugar was Cuba's chief export, and the United States had been the main customer. Now the U.S. cut off sugar imports from Cuba. Castro turned to the Soviet Union for help, and a trade agreement was reached.

President Dwight D. Eisenhower's administration severed all diplomatic ties with Cuba on January 3, 1961. Around this time he also authorized the Central Intelligence Agency (CIA) to draw up plans for an invasion by U.S.-trained anti-Castro Cuban forces. The invasion took place at the Bay of Pigs in April 1961, after President John F. Kennedy took office. It was a complete disaster. In its aftermath, Cuba forged a closer relationship with the Soviet Union.

NIKITA GOES TO HOLLYWOOD

During the late 1950s, Khrushchev had also been concerned with the Soviet Union's role in outer space. The Soviets had launched a rocket that had sailed past the moon at a speed of 5,500 miles an hour and was going into permanent orbit around the Sun. The 3,328-pound device was loaded with a variety of measuring instruments capable of transmitting information back to Earth. Once again the Soviet Union had pulled ahead of the United States in space exploration.

In September 1959, Khrushchev visited the United States. The first Soviet leader to ever set foot on U.S. soil, he met with President Eisenhower. At Camp David, the presidential retreat, they discussed the mass migration of people from Communist East Berlin to American-occupied West Berlin. Between 1949 and 1961, the number of Germans who crossed over reached 2.8 million. The two leaders were both gentle and frank with each other. Khrushchev agreed with Eisenhower that the Berlin situation was "abnormal" and that "human affairs got very badly tangled at times."[3] They parted, agreeing to continue seeking a solution at a summit meeting in Paris in the spring of 1960.

Following the Camp David meeting, Khrushchev embarked on a whirlwind tour of the United States, which ended in Hollywood. On the set of the film *Can Can* he expressed shock at the gyrations of a chorus of energetic female dancers. Later, he blew his top when he was told it would be too dangerous for him to visit Disneyland. "What is it?" he exploded. "Do you have rocket launching pads there? Is there an epidemic of cholera there or something? Or have gangsters taken hold of the place that can destroy me?"[4]

SOLIDARITY FORSAKEN

Shortly after his visit to the United States, Khrushchev went to China for another meeting with Chairman Mao. The first topic they discussed was the ongoing border dispute between China and India, which was threatening to grow into a war. Khrushchev was still cultivating a friendly relationship with India, the world's most populous nonaligned country. He made an ongoing effort to keep it out of the sphere of influence of the United States. Now, in a mocking tone, he told Mao that a few kilometers of territory one way or the other "are not important." Then, referring to the Chinese occupation of Tibet, Khrushchev criticized them for letting the Tibetan leader, the Dalai Lama, slip through their fingers. "It would have been better," he said, "if he'd been put in his coffin."[5]

Mao replied angrily. He accused Khrushchev of kowtowing to the United States. Then Khrushchev lost his temper, shouting that "we hold a principled Communist position. You want to subject us to yourselves," he added, "but you won't succeed." Chen Yi, one of Mao's top advisers, responded that "I am indignant at your statement that the worsening of relations is our fault." Khrushchev said that he, too, was indignant and that if Comrade Chen Yi truly believed he was not acting in good faith, "then don't offer me your hand, because I won't shake it."[6]

The meeting marked the end of China's belief in the Soviet Union as the source of authority for all Communist governments. Later Khrushchev remarked that Chairman Mao "was bursting with an impatient desire to rule the world."[7] What had been an alliance was now a competition for

CHAPTER SIX

THE BRINK OF WAR

> **It shall be the policy of this nation to regard any nuclear missile launched from Cuba against any nation in the Western Hemisphere as an attack by the Soviet Union on the United States, requiring a full retaliatory response upon the Soviet Union. . . . I call upon Chairman Khrushchev to halt and eliminate this clandestine, reckless, and provocative threat to world peace. . . . He has an opportunity now to move the world back from the abyss of destruction.**
>
> President John F. Kennedy alerts the nation to the Cuban missile crisis in an October 22, 1962, television address

The Berlin Wall began as a barbed-wire fence erected on the Sunday morning of August 13, 1961. Strung along the border between East and West Berlin by East German laborers working under armed guards, the line of the fence zigzagged through avenues, cemeteries, and apartment complexes. It blocked border crossings like the famed Brandenburg Gate. On Monday, East Berlin workers trying to get to their jobs in West Berlin were turned back by East German police, told "the border is closed," and forcibly dispersed.[1] Over the next few weeks, work gangs under military supervision replaced the fence with a 6-foot-high wall topped by barbed wire to prevent its being climbed over. The wall was studded with gun positions and tank traps.

At this time defections from East Germany through East Berlin to West Berlin had mounted to two thousand a day. The wall was built to stop them. Crossing over to West Berlin was now forbidden by the Soviet-installed East German Communist government. The edict was backed up by troops with instructions to shoot to kill anyone who attempted to disobey it.

The Berlin Wall was a Cold War symbol that for twenty-eight years separated East and West Berlin, preventing people from leaving East Germany. This 1961 photo shows its early construction.

Nevertheless, many did, with mixed results. Peter Fechter was shot while trying to escape across the wall. He straddled the wall for hours before he bled to death. Some East Berlin tenements had rear windows extending over the wall and into West Berlin. One fifty-nine-year-old woman threw a mattress out of her window and leaped after it. She died from her injuries. When someone prepared to jump from one of these windows, West Berlin firemen would try to catch them with blankets. On one occasion, as newsreel cameras rolled, East Berlin police tried to drag back a woman attempting to jump through the window of her apartment while West Berlin firemen with ladders tried to pull her to safety. When the woman was rescued, a West Berlin crowd cheered loudly.

THE BERLIN STANDOFF

The Berlin Wall provoked responses and counterresponses. A 1,500-strong American combat unit was dispatched to West Berlin to reinforce its garrison. There had been eighty crossing points from East Berlin prior to the wall. Now the Communists allowed only seven, and these were carefully monitored. Only one of the seven allowed crossings from West to East Berlin. This crossing was known as Checkpoint Charlie where Americans and Soviets exchanged captured spies.

American General Lucius D. Clay ordered the construction of a concrete wall at an army training camp so that soldiers could practice knocking it down. Under the joint occupation agreement, Americans were to have free access to East Berlin. When one group was harassed at Checkpoint Charlie by East German border guards, Clay ordered American jeeps guarded by squads of armed soldiers to escort visiting westerners into East Berlin. The soldiers were under orders to flaunt their weapons and hang tough. Ten American tanks were pulled up outside Checkpoint Charlie.

On October 27, 1961, thirty-three Soviet tanks pulled up at the Brandenburg Gate. Ten more Soviet tanks formed a line at Checkpoint Charlie. Their cannons were raised and aimed at the American tanks a mere hundred yards away. The American gunners loaded their cannons and waited for orders. The U.S. garrison in West Berlin was put on full alert. NATO and the Strategic Air Command followed suit.

The Red Army commander called Khrushchev. The Soviet leader told him he must respond with force if the Americans used force. American units were operating under similar orders. Commanders on both sides feared that a nervous soldier might fire a shot and start a firefight that could escalate into a third world war.

President Kennedy contacted Khrushchev. He told him that if the Soviets pulled back, the Americans would follow suit. Khrushchev agreed in principle, but the actual withdrawal was delicate. One Soviet tank backed up five yards. A few minutes passed. Then an American tank pulled back. One after another, the tanks of both forces withdrew. In the aftermath, Kennedy ordered American civilians not to visit East Berlin. Khrushchev, while still arrogant publicly, privately observed that "steps which would exacerbate the situation, especially in Berlin, should be avoided."[2] Conflict had been averted, but during the Cold War, further face-offs were a certainty.

A THREAT IS BORN

Khrushchev's desire to avoid confrontation didn't last long. His Cold War policy was never consistent, moving frequently from conciliation to confrontation. In early 1962 he decided "it was high time America learned what it feels like to have her own land and her own people threatened."[3] He looked to Cuba as the means to accomplish this.

The failed Bay of Pigs invasion sponsored by the United States had enraged Khrushchev. After all, Cuba was the major anti-imperialist force in the Western Hemisphere. What right had the United States to attempt to overthrow its government? When Cuban leader Fidel Castro asked the Soviet Union to support Cuba "against attacks and threats of military attack on our country by the United States," Khrushchev responded positively.[4] He saw it as an opportunity to challenge the Jupiter IRBM missiles the United States had deployed in Turkey and Iran. If the United States could aim missiles at the USSR from neighboring countries, why shouldn't the USSR do likewise by positioning missiles on Cuban territory?

So it was that in early 1962, Khrushchev okayed the installation by Soviet technicians of thirty-six medium-range ballistic missiles and twenty-four intermediate-range ballistic missiles on the island of Cuba. These missiles had a range of between 1,000 and 2,200 nautical miles. They were to be equipped with nuclear warheads and could easily strike most major American cities. Fifty-thousand Soviet servicemen sailed to Cuba to install and man the missiles.

THE CUBAN MISSILES

The operation was called Anadyr, and it proceeded in absolute secrecy. Shipments to Cuba began in the middle of July from a number of Soviet ports. Everything from skis and sheepskins to farm machinery and tractors were loaded onto the ships to disguise the real cargoes of missile components and warheads. The ships set sail for ports in Africa and South America, and only when they were far out at sea were sealed instructions opened by the ships' captains redirecting them to Cuba. They were outfitted with artillery to defend themselves if they were stopped for any reason. Each captain's orders were "to sink the ship" rather than allow it to be boarded.[5] At various times some sixty-nine torpedo-armed Soviet submarines escorted the ships with instructions to torpedo any vessel that attempted to intercept them.

On October 14 an American U-2 spy plane first spotted the Soviet missiles being assembled in Cuba. The next day McGeorge Bundy, the national security adviser, informed President Kennedy. Horrified, Kennedy said it was "just as if we suddenly began to put a major number of [missiles] in Turkey."[6] An adviser reminded him that we had indeed done precisely that.

President Kennedy convened the Executive Committee of the National Security Council (ExComm) to appraise the crisis. Those present were unanimous that the missiles must be removed. The question was whether the missile site could be effectively bombed, or whether some other option was possible. If it was bombed, would the Soviets retaliate?

At first the president favored bombing Cuba. Air Force General Curtis LeMay informed him that to be successful, the bombing would have to involve "a major air offensive . . . with hundreds of bombing sorties."[7] The ExComm broke into two factions: hawks, who favored a massive surprise bombing attack; and doves, who favored a diplomatic approach to either Castro, Khrushchev, or both. The debate went on over the next few days.

On October 18, President Kennedy met with Andrei Gromyko, the Soviet foreign minister. Gromyko insisted that Soviet military assistance to Cuba was purely defensive. Kennedy decided not to reveal that he knew about the missiles until the question of bombing was resolved with ExComm. Gromyko was sure he had lulled Kennedy's suspicions of Soviet intentions. "There is reason to believe that the United States has no current plans for an invasion of Cuba," he wired Khrushchev.[8]

That evening, ExComm learned that the installation of medium-range missiles in Cuba was nearly complete and that they could be launched within eighteen hours. At this point a third option, in addition to bombing and diplomacy, was raised. This was a plan for a naval blockade, to be called a quarantine, which would involve intercepting and searching all Soviet ships bound for Cuba, and preventing those carrying any sort of missile components, or arms, from delivering their cargoes to the island. This would be followed up by a demand that the Soviets remove the missiles from Cuba.

THE FACE-OFF

On October 22, Kennedy informed the nation that "a number of launchpads for offensive missiles are being built" by the Soviet Union on Cuba. This was how Khrushchev learned that the United States knew about the missiles. Kennedy also announced the naval quarantine of Cuba. It went into effect two days later. Khrushchev responded that if the United States provoked a nuclear war, the USSR "would carry out the most powerful retaliatory strike."[9]

The Soviets had the power to do this. It was estimated that between 20 and 25 percent of Soviet missiles could strike American targets. Ten to twelve American cities would fall victim to nuclear bombs. Armed forces of both countries were put on full battle readiness. Both Khrushchev and Kennedy were contemplating actions of mass destruction.

A letter from Kennedy was transmitted to Khrushchev on October 25. It justified the quarantine because all Soviet assurances to the contrary "were false and your forces have recently begun establishing a complex of

President John F. Kennedy announces
a naval blockade of Cuba until Soviet ballistic
missiles installed there in 1962 are removed.

develop an atomic bomb. The Chinese viewed this as a violation of the treaty of mutual technical assistance the two countries had signed. In 1962 the Soviets had withheld support from China when it waged a border war against India. Furthermore, hostility between Khrushchev and Chairman Mao had hardened since their acrimonious meeting in 1959. Khrushchev spoke of Mao as one whose "chauvinism and arrogance sent a shiver up my spine."[3]

Mao had been quick to criticize Khrushchev's handling of the Cuban missile crisis. Officials of the Chinese government had publicly called Khrushchev "foolish for placing missiles in Cuba and cowardly for removing them."[4] By September 1963 even more harsh accusations were being exchanged. The Soviets charged that the Chinese had "betrayed" the international Communist cause.[5] The Chinese accused the Soviets of supporting "antiparty elements in the Chinese Communist party," meaning critics of Chairman Mao.[6] The Soviets charged the Chinese with provoking some five thousand border violations. The Chinese pointed out that the border territories in question had been stolen from their country by a Russian tsar.

Khrushchev had reason to be concerned. From his point of view, 600 or 700 million Chinese ruled by a warmonger like Mao who now renounced Soviet Communist leadership amounted to a major threat. The Chinese had nuclear plants and designs on Soviet territory. They didn't have an atomic bomb yet, but they would surely have one soon. The unspoken question was whether the Soviet Union should bomb China's nuclear plants before the Chinese had an atomic bomb that could be used against them.

FUMBLES AND FAILURES

The Chinese were not the only ones who criticized Khrushchev's actions in Cuba. High-ranking members of both his own government and the Soviet military were muttering that Khrushchev had almost pushed the USSR into a nuclear war in Cuba, and then had backed down and allowed the Americans to humiliate the Soviet Union. Nor was Cuba the only source of dissatisfaction with Khrushchev's leadership. There were many Khrushchev policies that had failed and were now causing hardship.

His program for promoting the growth of heavy industry, at first successful, had fallen off badly in 1963 and 1964. Farm production had also dropped, and the USSR faced serious food shortages. Khrushchev tried to alleviate these by buying 150 million bushels of wheat from the United States. That had relieved the situation, but hard-line Communists were outraged at the USSR becoming a trading partner of a capitalist country.

Khrushchev had cut back on appropriations for the military, and this had also increased the hard-liners' opposition to him. Back in 1957 he had created local economic councils, but they hadn't worked out. When he now combined them so that there were fewer councils, and reassigned their duties and powers, the result caused great confusion. The officials involved now joined those who questioned Khrushchev's decisions.

He even managed to alienate those he had raised to positions of power in the Soviet Communist party. He had pushed through a rule limiting the terms of party officials. Ever the practical politician, the rule enabled him to promote people to key positions while stopping them from holding those positions long enough to amass enough power to be a threat to him. He had in effect taken away their job security, and their resentment became part of the opposition to his regime.

The ill-advised action that cost him the most political support occurred in the late autumn of 1962 when he split the Communist party in two, making one part responsible for industry, and the other for agriculture. This was supposed to create greater efficiency. It bombed. There were now two people in charge of each region instead of one. Their authority often overlapped. Underlings couldn't tell who was in charge. Health and education programs never got off the ground because responsibility for them was not assigned. The chaos the split created cost Khrushchev much of the popular support he had once enjoyed.

KHRUSHCHEV'S VISION

In November 1963, President John F. Kennedy had been assassinated. Vice President Lyndon Johnson had replaced him. American involvement in Vietnam had begun under Kennedy and was continuing under Johnson. However, the American people were not yet focused on it to the extent that they would be during the coming months and years. Nor was Khrushchev focused on Vietnam. The leader of North Vietnam, Ho Chi Minh, was a Moscow-trained Communist, but Khrushchev was not going to let that interfere with his plans to forge bonds for peace with America.

Throughout 1964, Khrushchev's main concern was the upcoming United States presidential election. The missile crisis had left Khrushchev feeling that he and Kennedy could work together for peace. The assassination had been a shattering blow to him, but he found that Johnson also seemed committed to peace. Johnson's reelection was imperative. If his right-wing and militantly anti-Communist Republican rival Senator Barry Goldwater beat Johnson, it would wreck Khrushchev's desire to firm up a friendly relationship with the United States.

Before the election, Khrushchev sent his son-in-law Alexei Adzhubei to Bonn, West Germany. According to Edward Crankshaw, a correspondent covering Moscow for *The Observor*, a London newspaper, and the author of many books on Russia, Khrushchev was "preparing the great coup which would convince American opinion of his good intentions and cut the ground from under Senator Goldwater's feet. He was moving to an accommodation with West Germany. . . . He had a vision, and he was going to act on his vision."[7]

EXIT KHRUSHCHEV

It was not a vision shared by Khrushchev's colleagues. It was not so much that they disagreed with him as that they no longer had any faith in his judgment. They laughed at him behind his back and made up jokes about him. More kindly, they questioned whether his mind, at age seventy, was functioning as sharply as the mind of the leader of a great nation should function.

In early October 1964, Khrushchev went on vacation. There had been rumors of a plot to remove him from office, but he didn't take them seriously. But the resolve of the plotters grew in his absence. On October 12 he received a call from Leonid Brezhnev, who, until very recently, had served as chairman of the Presidium of the Supreme Soviet and had worked very closely with Khrushchev. Brezhnev had resigned that post,

A smiling Leonid Brezhnev (foreground) waves good-bye as
Nikita Khrushchev leaves for a vacation along the Black Sea. In his
absence, Brehznev and other party officials arrange to remove him
from power, and force Khrushchev to resign in October 1964.

always brightly polished."³ Both had cultivated a surface charm and amiability. Although Brezhnev was regarded by his contemporaries as "an obvious mediocrity" who rose to prominence because of "the need of opposing sides to exploit his weaknesses," he nevertheless dominated the more intelligent Kosygin.⁴

The pair were born within two years of each other in the early 1900s. Kosygin grew up in St. Petersburg, and although his father was a workingman, the younger Kosygin absorbed much of the culture and sophistication of the cosmopolitan capital of tsarist Russia. He joined the Red Army at the age of fifteen, and fought in several of the campaigns of the Russian civil war. Brezhnev was the son of a Ukrainian steel mill worker, and at the age of fifteen, he too went to work in the mill. He had little education, and little contact with the arts and literature. When he was seventeen, Brezhnev joined the Communist Youth League.

Both men survived, and then flourished, during the Stalinist purges of the 1930s. By the end of the decade, Kosygin had been named mayor of Leningrad (formerly St. Petersburg), as well as elected to the Central Committee of the Communist party. Brezhnev was elected deputy mayor of Dneprodzerzhinsk, a major Ukrainian industrial center with iron, steel, and chemical plants, and an important port on the Dnieper River. Here he became associated with Khrushchev, who had been sent to the Ukraine by Stalin to purge the top Ukrainian Communist party leadership.

As a loyal follower of Khrushchev's, Brezhnev served directly under him as a political officer with the rank of major general during World War II. After the war, he followed Khrushchev to Moscow and was eventually appointed first secretary of the Moldavian Communist party with the job of collectivizing agriculture in Moldavia. During the war, Kosygin had remained in Leningrad. In 1942 he led 500,000 people from the besieged city across frozen Lake Lagoda to safety. At war's end, Stalin appointed Kosygin minister of finance. In that post, Kosygin succeeded in stabilizing the nation's finances.

Kosygin and Brezhnev both supported Khrushchev's rise to power after Stalin's death. Both endorsed his policies and were considered Khrushchev loyalists. Yet both men were leaders of the coup that deposed Khrushchev in 1964.

Kosygin's government programs were subject to implementation by the Soviet Communist party. Brezhnev controlled the party through a system of rewards and punishments. Kosygin had the title of premier, but Brezhnev was in charge. The years of his rule became known as the Brezhnev era. In the United States, those years roughly corresponded to the period of the Vietnam War.

Vietnam had been a French colony until after World War II when a rebellion led by Russian-trained Communist Ho Chi Minh drove the French from the country. It ended with an agreement signed in Geneva, Switzerland, on July 21, 1954, which divided the country into North and South Vietnam. A Communist government led by Ho Chi Minh was formed in North Vietnam. The United States supported an anti-Communist regime in South Vietnam.

The Geneva agreement stipulated that elections be held to unify the country. Afraid that the Communists would take over, the United States blocked the elections. American policy makers believed that if Vietnam went Communist, it would provoke a series of Communist rebellions in Southeast Asia that might extend to the Philippines and even to Hawaii. This was the domino theory, which determined subsequent American actions in Vietnam.

When the Viet Cong (South Vietnamese rebels backed by North Vietnam), began a guerilla war to overthrow the South Vietnamese government, the United States acted. Between 1962 and 1963, President Kennedy dispatched 17,000 U.S. troops labeled "noncombat advisers" to Vietnam to train the army of South Vietnam.[5] In August 1964, following an attack by the North Vietnamese on two U.S. destroyers, Congress passed the Gulf of Tonkin resolution authorizing President Lyndon Johnson to take any action necessary to oppose North Vietnamese aggression. Congress had been told that the attack was unprovoked. It was later revealed that the two American ships had been actively aiding South Vietnamese military operations against the North Vietnamese. The Gulf of Tonkin resolution gave Johnson the authority to increase the number of American troops in Vietnam whenever he thought it necessary. He eventually dispatched more than 540,000 American soldiers there. More than 50,000 of them died before the war ended in 1975.

During the thirteen years it lasted, the Vietnam War was a major foreign policy concern for Brezhnev and Kosygin. They wanted to pursue the policy of "peaceful coexistence" with the United States that Khrushchev had instituted following the Cuban missile crisis. However, Communist North Vietnam was a potential satellite, which could provide a Soviet foothold in Asia. If the Soviet Union withheld aid from them, there was the danger that the North Vietnamese would end up in the Chinese camp. This would have threatened Soviet supremacy in the world Communist movement.

Following the passing of the Gulf of Tonkin resolution, the Soviets substantially increased their aid to North Vietnam and the Viet Cong. This assistance was primarily military, and between 1963 and 1967, it exceeded 1.8 billion rubles (the Soviet currency). It included the most modern surface-to-air missiles, jet planes, rockets, field artillery, and a variety of sophisticated arms and combat hardware. However, the North Vietnamese continued receiving aid from the Chinese as well, and refused to support the USSR in its ongoing border disputes with China.[6]

THE CULTURAL REVOLUTION

"Detente" is the word used to describe a lessening of tensions and hostilities between nations. It was increasingly applied to Soviet-U.S. relations during the Brezhnev era. This was in spite of the Vietnam conflict and because of the widening split between the Soviet Union and China. Despite ideological differences, the Soviets began to regard the United States as potentially accommodating, and China as a dangerously hostile rival.

These attitudes prevailed for the Soviets following the launching of the Great Proletarian Cultural Revolution in China during the spring of 1966. Similar to the Stalinist purges in the Soviet Union during the 1930s, the purpose of the Cultural Revolution was to get rid of anyone in the Chinese government and society whose ideas ran counter to those of Chairman Mao. Schools and artistic organizations were purged of all "bourgeois reactionary thinking." In government-sponsored demonstrations the Maoists carried posters of Mao and Stalin, and shouted slogans attacking "Soviet revisionism and U.S. imperialism." Mao's fervent followers recited his latest poem:

> *Seize the day, seize the hour!*
> *Away with all the pests!*
> *Our force is irresistible!"* [7]

Soon the Cultural Revolution deteriorated into battles between rival Chinese factions. More than 60,000 prisoners were taken by both sides. The prisoners repeatedly underwent torture in which they had "fingers and noses chopped off." It wasn't until February 1967 that Mao succeeded in reestablishing his control over the country. [8]

Four months later, in June 1967, Premier Kosygin met with President Johnson in Glassboro, New Jersey. They avoided the subject of the Vietnam War, disagreed about how to achieve peace in the Middle East, and argued over whether Soviet antiballistic missiles were "defensive" weapons. [9] Although they reached no conclusions on arms control, the discussions were friendly, and laid the groundwork for future talks, which would be more productive. Both leaders worried that the recent explosion of a hydrogen bomb by China would affect the chances of reaching an agreement on arms limitation.

PRAGUE SPRING

Toward the end of 1967, leaders in the Communist bloc country of Czechoslovakia began demanding democratic reforms. In January 1968, the Czech Communist party elected Alexander Dubcek as first secretary. According to KGB (Soviet secret police) reports that Brezhnev was receiving, Dubcek had "counter-revolutionary tendencies," and would pursue a foreign policy independent of the Soviet Union. [10]

"Prague Spring" began in April. It was launched by Dubcek with the phrase "socialism with a human face." [11] For the first time since the beginning of World War II, there were open debates going on in the central squares of the capital city of Prague. Students protested Soviet control of

A Czech citizen walks past graffiti equating the Soviet occupation of Czechoslovakia with U.S. policy in Vietnam, as a Russian soldier lights his cigarette.

their country. Horror stories were told publicly about the excesses of the secret police and the beatings in the work camps.

By June, Brezhnev had ordered Soviet troops stationed in Poland and East Germany to deploy on the Czech border. Brezhnev and Kosygin notified Dubcek that he must stop pursuing democratic reforms. He ignored their demands. On July 30 two fresh Soviet divisions equipped with tanks, artillery, and rockets were also dispatched to the Czech border.

Czechoslovakia was invaded by several hundred thousand Soviet troops on August 20. A massive airlift brought tanks and soldiers into Prague. Soviet planes filled the skies over the city. When the Soviets stormed the major radio station in Prague, a battle followed. Thirty Czechs were killed and three hundred more were injured. On September 13, Dubcek capitulated to the Soviet demands and agreed to curtail his democratic programs. He agreed to outlaw all political parties except the Communists, and to follow Moscow's policies. Liberals would be excluded from the government, and the media would be put under strict government control. Soviet troops would be permanently stationed in Czechoslovakia.

THE BREZHNEV DOCTRINE

The invasion was justified by the Soviets with the Brezhnev Doctrine, which proclaimed that "every Communist party" in every country "is responsible not only to its own people but also to all the Socialist countries and to the entire Communist movement." In other words, political behavior was to serve the "fundamental interest" of world communism as defined in Moscow, rather than that of one particular country. It warned that the Soviet Union would not allow any Communist country to revert to capitalism. The Brezhnev Doctrine would influence Soviet foreign policy over the next decade.[12]

U.S. government protests over the Soviet invasion of Czechoslovakia were muted. The anti-Vietnam war movement was at its peak and protesters were filling the parks and streets of Chicago, where the 1968 Democratic National Convention was being held. As Soviet tanks and troops occupied Prague, in Chicago armed national guardsmen with mobile weapons carriers and local police with billy clubs were dispersing

American demonstrators while a shocked nation watched on television. As tear-gas canisters exploded, the victims chanted "Prague! Prague! Prague! Prague!"[13] It was difficult for our government to be indignant about Prague while the chaos of Chicago filled the TV screens.

Nor did Brezhnev capitalize on the disruptions in the United States. The opportunity was there for antidemocratic propaganda, but he didn't take it. His aim was still detente. Yet Soviet policy was inconsistent. Even as Brezhnev made overtures to reduce tensions with the United States, he was aggressively building up the stockpile of Soviet weapons. Between 1966 and 1970, Soviet military spending almost doubled. During the first four years of Brezhnev's reign, the stockpile of Soviet intercontinental ballistic missiles (ICBMs) grew from 190 to 860. Missiles designed for launching from submarines increased from 29 to 120. Brezhnev built the Soviet navy into a major force. By the end of the 1960s, USSR military power equaled—and may even have surpassed—that of the United States.

THE BREZHNEV
ERA (2)

> **Perhaps the key problem for us today is to tighten discipline. Both in the state and among labour . . . the tightening of discipline must be done across the board . . .**
>
> In a speech to the Politburo on September 9, 1982, shortly before his death, Leonid Brezhnev suggested a solution to the Soviet Union's economic crisis

In March 1969, Soviet troops occupied the island of Chenpao in the middle of the frozen Ussuri River on the border between the USSR and China. The Chinese charged that the Soviets were using the island to launch artillery attacks "deep within Chinese territory" in Manchuria, a Chinese province with a disputed border between it and Soviet Siberia. After a Chinese counterattack killed thirty-one of their soldiers, the Soviets attacked Chinese border posts with "armored vehicles, tanks and armed troops." In August, the two countries fought a major battle along the frontier.[1]

A strange war of words erupted during the fighting. In May 1970 when Moscow accused Chairman Mao of trying to establish rule over all of Asia, Mao responded by calling for world revolution against United States imperialism. On July 2 relations between the Soviet Union and China suddenly got better. The border dispute was settled, and for the first time since 1966, the two countries exchanged ambassadors.

The mysterious resolution of Soviet-Chinese differences reflected Brezhnev's conflicting policies. In many ways a tyrant, he nevertheless seemed to have a genuine commitment to seeking peace. For years the sticking point between the Soviet Union and the United States had been

Berlin, but in the summer of 1970, Brezhnev met with West German Chancellor Willy Brandt. The two arrived at agreements to increase trade and to stabilize Berlin. This was followed up by meetings later that year. In 1971 Brezhnev and Brandt signed a nonaggression pact, boundary agreements, and a friendship treaty. These were major stepping-stones to Soviet-American detente, or an easing of tensions between the two nations.

THE REFUSENIKS

That detente was often derailed by issues of social justice. This was the case in Poland just before Christmas 1970. A depressed economy controlled by the Soviets had caused a drastic rise in prices for food, fuel, and clothing, which resulted in a week of rioting. Demands that the Polish Communist party chief Wladyslaw Gomulka be dismissed were met with bullets. Sixty people were killed and hundreds were injured. After protests from many countries including the United States, the demonstrators' demands were met and Gomulka was dismissed.

That year ended with the conviction of eleven Soviet citizens for attempting to hijack a plane in an effort to escape tyranny and religious oppression. Nine of the eleven were Jews. Two were sentenced to death. At the same time, twenty other Jews were arrested throughout the Soviet Union on a variety of charges. After protests from around the world, the sentences of the hijackers were reduced.

Soviet policy severely restricted Jewish religious practices. Hebrew was a forbidden language. Jewish religious schools were banned. There were only sixty-two synagogues in the Soviet Union and they were prevented from forming a central Jewish organization. Rabbis were dying out, and the Soviets would not permit the opening of institutions to train their successors. The notation "Entry no. 5," stamped on all Jewish passports, identified the holders as Jews forbidden to leave the country.[2]

Emigration of Jews from the Soviet Union became a key issue linked to relations with the United States. Soviet Jews, calling themselves "refuseniks," began staging mass demonstrations to force the government to allow them to emigrate to Israel.[3] In February 1971, Soviet Jews organized a mass sit-in at the Supreme Soviet building in Moscow. This came at a time when the United States and the USSR were engaged in Strategic Arms Limitation Talks (SALT). The talks had begun in Helsinki, Finland, in November 1969. Now many members of Congress tied their approval of any arms agreement to the Soviets granting the right of emigration to Jews. The Soviets relented. Throughout 1971 and 1972, they allowed Jewish emigration to increase dramatically. In 1973 over 33,000 Jews were permitted to leave the USSR. That year, when Congress was considering granting the Soviet Union most-favored nation trade status, Senator Henry Jackson of Washington led a fight to make such status dependent on Moscow's relaxing its policies preventing Jewish emigration. Similar steps led to over 50,000 Jews being allowed to emigrate in 1979.

SALT I & SALT II

Throughout the 1970s, detente remained a major goal for Brezhnev. Although President Richard Nixon had built his political career on anti-communism, he proved a willing partner in striving for detente. Nixon went to the Soviet Union to meet with Brezhnev in May 1972. During his visit they signed an interim agreement known as SALT I. It included an antiballistic missile (ABM) treaty and an Interim Offensive Forces Agreement. SALT I limited each country's number of ABM sites, launchers, and missiles, froze the deployment of offensive intercontinental ballistic missiles (ICBMs), and "prohibited the testing or building of mobile land-based, space-based, air-based, or sea-based missile defenses."[4]

In November 1972, SALT meetings resumed with the aim of limiting multiple warhead missile (MIRV) systems. A formula was developed to limit the number of warheads on missiles. However, SALT II bogged down over Soviet testing of MIRVs and U.S. development of long-range cruise missiles. Between the time President Gerald Ford replaced Nixon in 1973, and the 1976 election campaign, negotiations ground to a halt. The Soviets were waiting to see with whom they would be negotiating as president. Jimmy Carter was elected president in 1976 and suggested changes to what had previously been discussed. Soviet foreign minister Andrei Gromyko publicly rebuked him. Finally, however, a SALT II agreement was signed by Carter and Brezhnev on June 18, 1979.

The United States Senate did not immediately ratify SALT II. In August 1979 it was learned that the Soviets had a combat brigade in Cuba. Idaho Senator Frank Church announced that SALT II would not be affirmed until the Soviet troops were removed. Before that happened, in December 1979, the Soviet Union invaded Afghanistan. U.S. reaction effectively killed SALT II.

AFGHANISTAN: LAND OF TURMOIL

Afghanistan was a landlocked country bordered by various Soviet Socialist Republics with mainly Muslim populations, as well as by Iran and Pakistan. One of the poorest and most backward countries in the world, Afghanistan had no natural resources of any value. At the end of the 1970s, Iran was in the process of being taken over by a powerful fundamentalist Muslim movement committed to spreading its doctrine to other Muslim lands. This endangered Communist authority in the region. To the United States, Afghanistan was a buffer nation between the Soviet Union and the strategically crucial oil-rich countries of the Persian Gulf. It followed that Afghanistan, with some of the most rugged terrain in the world, became a bone of contention between the United States and the Soviet Union.

In 1973 the king of Afghanistan had been overthrown by his cousin, Mohammed Daoud Khan. The United States, attempting to bring Afghanistan under its influence, had offered the new government aid for economic development. When the Soviets sent advisers to Afghanistan and established a Communist party there, Daoud Khan banned the party and deported the advisers. In 1977, Daoud Khan broke with Moscow altogether. A year later, Daoud Khan "was deposed and murdered in a coup led by Soviet-trained Afghan officers."[5]

A pro-Soviet regime took over in Afghanistan. However, Afghanistan's fundamentalist Islamic clerics, called mullahs, regarded communism as ungodly. With help from the recently installed fundamentalist government in Iran, they staged an armed uprising in the Afghan city of Herat. Hundreds of Afghans, along with Soviet advisers and their families, were killed by fundamentalist fanatics called mujahadeen. Their bodies were paraded through the streets.

A group of Afghan rebels proudly displays captured Soviet tank artillery shells after a raid on the town of Herat.

The Afghanistan government appealed to the Soviets: "The situation is bad and getting worse. We need practical help in both men and weapons."[6] Moscow responded by sending helicopter gunships and seven hundred paratroopers disguised as aircraft technicians to Kabul, the capital city of Afghanistan. Three Soviet divisions were deployed on the Afghanistan border.

THE CARTER DOCTRINE

In September 1979 the pro-Soviet Afghan president Nur Mohammed Taraki met with Brezhnev in Moscow to request additional aid. Upon his return, three of his political enemies murdered Taraki by suffocating him with a pillow. He was replaced by Hafizullah Amin, a military strongman whom Moscow feared might make a deal with the Americans, or—worse still—with Pakistan, an ally of Communist China.

On December 12, 1979, the Politburo met to decide what to do about the Afghanistan situation. Brezhnev, whose health had been failing, was drunk when he arrived. He kissed everyone before he sat down. When Amin's name was mentioned, he shouted, "Dirty man!" and stormed out of the room.[7] In his absence the Politburo decided to intervene militarily in Afghanistan. On Christmas day, hundreds of Soviet tanks and tens of thousands of motorized infantry crossed the border into Afghanistan.

Three days later President Carter labeled the Soviet invasion a "clear threat" to peace and told Brezhnev it "could mark a fundamental and long-lasting turning point in our relations."[8] He followed this up with what would come to be known as the Carter Doctrine, which stated that "an attempt by any outside force to gain control of the Persian Gulf region will be regarded as an assault on the vital interests of the United States of America, and such an assault will be repelled by any means necessary, including military force."[9]

Substantial U.S. arms shipments for the mujahadeen, routed through Pakistan, followed the warning. The mujahadeen were fighting a guerilla war, and as the Soviet Union poured more troops into Afghanistan, the mujahadeen massacred them and vanished into the caves and the hills without engaging in any major battles. The invasion turned into a war that would drag on for many years, but in the end the mujahadeen would prevail. The Soviets would withdraw. The mujahadeen would establish the repressive regime in Afghanistan known as the Taliban.

THE BEGINNING OF THE END

As the Afghanistan situation was heating up in October 1980, ill health forced Alexei Kosygin to resign as premier of the Soviet Union. On December 18 he died of a heart attack. Kosygin had been trying to undo the harm done to the Soviet economy by Khrushchev's domestic policies. He had restored the authority of the government ministries decentralized by Khrushchev. He brought back the incentive system for industrial mid-level managers and for agricultural supervisors. He set up a government department responsible for pricing, which set prices for goods at realistic levels in keeping with the costs of production, labor, supply, and demand.

These reforms, however, failed. An entrenched government bureaucracy afraid of losing its power sabotaged many of them. Basically, Kosygin had tried to build a healthy economy on the foundation of an unhealthy one. As a result, the economy of the USSR had declined steadily throughout the 1960s and 1970s.

The peasant population of the Soviet Union was hit hardest. In 1939 two thirds of the people of the Soviet Union had worked on farms. By the end of the 1970s, that figure had been reduced to one quarter. As a result, there were ongoing food shortages. Sometimes, the discontent of the people erupted.

In Kiev in 1969 and Dnepropetrovsk in 1972, there had been demonstrations protesting poor housing. There had also been food riots in Sverdlovsk in 1969 and in Gorky in 1980. Harsh labor conditions had led to protests in Vitebsk in 1973 and Kiev in 1981. Long hours and low pay provoked walkouts in Togliatti in 1981. Police brutality brought on mass demonstrations in Alexandrov in 1969, Dneprodzerzhinsk in 1972, and Ordzhonikidze in 1981.

The people were reacting to the increasing hardships caused by the crumbling Soviet economy. The signs of decline had been there for all to see throughout the Brezhnev era. For eighteen years, Leonid Brezhnev had turned a blind eye to the system's failures. The situation was critical when he died in office, following a long illness, on November 10, 1982.

CHAPTER TEN

A DYING LEADERSHIP

> It is the Soviet Union that runs against the tide of history by denying human freedom and human dignity to its citizens. It also is in deep economic difficulty. The rate of growth in the national product has been steadily declining since the fifties and is less than half of what it was then. . . . The constant shrinkage of economic growth combined with the growth of military production is putting a heavy strain on the Soviet people.
>
> President Ronald Reagan's "Evil Empire" speech of June 8, 1982

If discontent was rising in the Soviet Union as the 1980s began, it was overflowing in its closest satellite, Poland. In August 1980 workers in the Gdansk shipyard formed a union called Solidarity, which would grow into a nationwide movement. Such nongovernment unions were forbidden in Poland. This one, led by Lech Walesa, an unemployed electrician, staged a walkout and began a seventeen-day strike. When twenty-eight of the strikers were jailed, protests swelled across the country and some 300,000 Polish workers engaged in work slowdowns.

The Polish government, despite still being subject to Soviet control, was forced to give in to the strikers' demands. Those in jail were released, work hours were shortened, and promises were made to improve working conditions. Most significantly, the government granted the right of workers to form independent unions and to strike.

The Soviets viewed this as a challenge to Communist discipline. Soviet troops massed on the Polish border. The North Atlantic Treaty Organization

(NATO) warned the Soviets that if they interfered in Poland, "the alliance would be compelled to react."[1]

SOLIDARITY PREVAILS

In January 1981, Solidarity workers walked off their jobs to back up a demand for a five-day work week. As the days went by, millions of Poles stopped working and joined the Solidarity movement. With the Soviet threat hovering over Poland, the government was thrown into turmoil. The prime minister was forced out of office and replaced by General Wojciech Jaruzelski. The military temporarily restored order, and Solidarity leader Lech Walesa was jailed. When the authorities arrested him, Walesa told them that "this is the moment of your defeat. These are the last nails in the coffin of communism."[2]

Despite the crackdown, the Solidarity movement grew throughout the spring and summer of 1981. Its rallies became openly anti-Soviet, and the government warned Solidarity that its actions were endangering the "independent existence" of Poland.[3] By mid-December, martial law had been imposed, and strikers in coal mines, shipyards, and factories were fighting pitched battles with police. Ten months later Solidarity was outlawed. Striking workers were drafted into military service and forced to return to work.

The repression lasted seven years. By that time, the Soviet domination of Eastern Europe was abating. Once again protests erupted in Poland. General Jaruzelski was forced to reopen talks with the banned Solidarity movement, now constituted as a political party. As a result, the first Polish free elections since World War II were held. In 1990, Lech Walesa won an overwhelming vote and became president of Poland.

ANDROPOV VS. REAGAN

Soviet threats to intervene in Poland in the mid-1980s had been quite serious. Detailed plans had been made for "Warsaw Pact military intervention" involving "fifteen Soviet, two Czech and one East German" divisions.[4] There were two reasons why there was no follow through on

Polish electrician Lech Walesa addresses a crowd of workers at a protest against that country's Communist government. The Solidarity trade union federation would be instrumental in bringing about free elections in Poland.

these plans. The first was the overextension of Soviet involvement in Afghanistan and the strain it was putting on the military. The second was the lack of any firmly established and lasting authority in the Soviet government, both during the illness preceding Brezhnev's death and for a long time afterward.

Brezhnev's eventual successor was sixty-eight-year-old Yuri Andropov, who had been head of the KGB for fifteen years. He was a conservative who had urged the 1968 invasion of Czechoslovakia and had persecuted dissident intellectuals like the writer Aleksandr Solzhenitzyn and the physicist Andrei Sakharov. In his first speech as the new Soviet leader in 1982, he lashed out at the Western powers, saying that "the imperialists will never meet one's pleas for peace."[5] It was a change from Brezhnev's speeches favoring detente.

Like Kosygin, Andropov tried to reorganize economic planning. Also like Kosygin, he was thwarted by an entrenched bureaucracy bent on protecting its privileges. Andropov was more successful in imposing a strict discipline and order on society at large. Absenteeism from work declined, the rate of alcoholism went down, and there was a brief surge in industrial productivity.

Andropov's first challenge from the United States came in March 1983 when President Ronald Reagan announced plans to build an invulnerable missile shield—the so-called Star Wars initiative. The Soviets feared that if it worked, Star Wars might render the Soviet nuclear arsenal useless. Also, building the shield would violate the ABM treaty of 1972. Andropov called the Reagan plan "insane" and "flippant" and "irresponsible."[6]

FLIGHT 007

Three months after taking office, Andropov was treated for kidney failure. From then on his health deteriorated rapidly. Nevertheless, he proved strong when it came to certain areas of Soviet foreign policy. The war in Afghanistan continued under his leadership. At the same time he carried on an anti-Israel policy, which supplied billions of dollars worth of aid to Arab countries such as Libya, Syria, and Iraq. Artillery systems, thousands of tanks, and hundreds of aircraft were exported to the Arab world.

Andropov, like his predecessors, viewed Israel as a United States outpost, and Israel's enemies as allies in the war against U.S. imperialism.

Andropov's negative attitude toward the United States, together with Reagan's Star Wars militancy, greatly hindered progress in the Strategic Arms Reduction Talks (START), which had been dragging on since 1982 with little progress. Both sides in the talks had made demands favorable to themselves knowing that the other side would reject them. Then, on August 31, 1983, something happened that resulted in the talks collapsing altogether.

Korean Air Lines flight 007, bound for Seoul from Alaska, strayed off course into Soviet air space. It flew near a Soviet secret missile test site on the Kamchatka Peninsula. A Soviet fighter plane shot down the airliner, killing all 269 people on board. Sixty-one of the passengers were Americans, including Georgia congressman Larry McDonald.

The Soviets did not reveal the fate of the aircraft until a week after it crashed. When they did, President Reagan called it an "act of barbarism."[7] The Soviets claimed that the plane was on a spying mission for the United States. Neither interpretation was quite true. Before the incident, a U.S. spy plane had, indeed, flown into Soviet air space to spy on the missile range. The Soviets had detected it and put their forces on high alert. The fighter pilot who shot down the Korean airliner had been relying on instruments, and assumed it was another spy plane. A report by the UN Civil Aviation Organization confirmed that the tragedy was a mistake.

Nevertheless, President Reagan persisted in condemning the Soviet Union for the tragedy. There was a practical political reason for this. There was opposition in Congress to an arms bill he supported. His outrage, he later confessed, "gave badly needed impetus in Congress to the rearmament programs." The Soviets reacted accordingly. On September 28, Andropov said the United States was following a "militarist course that represents a serious threat to peace." Soviet-U.S. antagonism was now intense.[8]

KONSTANTIN CHERNENKO

Relations had not improved by February 9, 1984, when Yuri Andropov died. His health had been failing for some time, and his hold on the Soviet government had also been slipping. The Politburo unanimously selected

Konstantin Chernenko to succeed Andropov as general secretary. At age seventy-two, Chernenko was three years older than Andropov at his death.

Konstantin Chernenko had been born into a peasant family in the Siberian village of Bolshaya Tes in 1911. He had little formal schooling, and at the age of eighteen joined the Communist Youth League (Komsomol). He volunteered for the army and served on the Chinese border until 1933, when he left the army to engage in propaganda activities for the Soviet Communist party. He continued this work throughout World War II, after which he enrolled in the Higher School for Party Organizers in Moscow. After his graduation, he was sent to the Soviet republic of Moldavia, where he served as party secretary for propaganda until 1956. Here he met Leonid Brezhnev and became his protégé. As Brezhnev rose in Soviet politics, so did Chernenko. During Brezhnev's eighteen-year rule, Chernenko advanced to become a full member of the Politburo, and also served in the Secretariat of the Communist party Central Committee, charged with running day-to-day party affairs.

Despite Chernenko's rise, Brezhnev's rivals regarded him as little more than Brezhnev's lackey. Foreign Minister Andrei Gromyko called Chernenko a "second-rate opportunist."[9] After Brezhnev's death, Chernenko had been passed over in favor of Andropov because he was identified with Brezhnev's failed domestic policies. The selection of the aging Chernenko to succeed Andropov was a temporary measure to fill a leadership void until someone more suitable could be agreed upon by the Soviet leadership.

THE REAGAN DOCTRINE

Chernenko's first foreign policy statements sent a mixed message. Calling for peaceful coexistence with the United States, he insisted that "we need no military superiority." But he also insisted that it was necessary that the Soviets stockpile nuclear weapons "to cool the hot heads of militant adventurists."[10]

Soon, however, the Soviet attitude hardened. This was a reaction to the so-called Reagan Doctrine, an increasingly hostile policy toward the Soviet Union characterized by President Reagan's statement that the United

States must support "the forces of freedom in Communist totalitarian states."[11] To the Soviets this meant that the United States might actively encourage rebellions in Eastern European countries, or perhaps even in the Soviet Union itself.

On May 8, 1984, the Soviet National Olympic Committee announced that the USSR would not take part in the Olympic Games scheduled for Los Angeles that summer. In part this was payback for the United States having boycotted the games in Moscow in 1980 in protest of the Soviet invasion of Afghanistan. The Soviets didn't refer directly to this. Instead, they claimed that "an anti-Soviet hysteria" was deliberately "being whipped up in the [United States]."[12] The implication was that the U.S. government was behind it.

PERESTROIKA AND GLASNOST

It's not clear what Chernenko's role was in deciding to boycott the Olympic Games. By autumn he was already becoming seriously ill. At meetings of the Politburo his emphysema often left him too short of breath to speak. He seemed to have difficulty focusing on issues, and often wavered between points of view, first siding with one faction, then the other. Sometimes after fifteen or twenty minutes, he would have to leave a meeting. Sometimes he would be too ill to attend at all.

In Chernenko's absence, the older members of the Politburo who had backed him found themselves falling under the spell of a dynamic young leader named Mikhail Gorbachev. In December 1984 Gorbachev gave a speech that attracted wide attention not just in the Politburo and the Soviet Union, but in the United States as well. He spoke of perestroika—a reconstruction of the Soviet system with implications of democracy—and of glasnost—the free dissemination of information, and an end to secrecy at home and abroad.

Soon a reform movement grew around Gorbachev. Four months after the glasnost speech, on March 10, 1985, Konstantin Chernenko died. He was the third Soviet leader to pass away in two and a half years. The politburo unanimously named Mikhail Gorbachev to replace him. It was the start of a new and dramatically different era in Soviet history.

GORBACHEV AND CHERNOBYL

> Any interference in domestic affairs of any kind, any attempts to limit the sovereignty of states, both of friends and allies, no matter whose it is, is impermissible.
>
> Mikhail Gorbachev confirms the end of the Brezhnev Doctrine to the Council of Europe

Mikhail Gorbachev was the first leader in the history of the Soviet Union who was not alive during the Russian Revolution. His comparative youth made a significant difference between him and the three aging leaders who preceded him. It was a difference that would change the course of his country's history and affect the future of the world.

RAISED IN TURMOIL

Born in the village of Privolnoye in the north of the Caucasus mountains on March 2, 1931, Mikhail Sergeyevich Gorbachev was the grandchild of committed Communists. Both of his grandfathers were caught up in the Stalinist purges of the 1930s and sent to prison camps. His maternal grandfather was beaten and tortured. Nevertheless, both were eventually released, and still remained Communists.

When Mikhail was ten years old the Germans invaded the Soviet Union, and Mikhail's father was drafted into the army. During the winter of 1941–1942, Privolnoye was snowed in and cut off from the outside world. It was a bitter time marked by cold, hunger, and physical hardship. The following summer, the German Army occupied Privolnoye. The Gorbachev family was warned that the Germans were going to round up

Communists and shoot them. The family fled, and eleven-year-old Mikhail was hidden on a farm outside the village. Not long after, the Soviet army liberated Provolnoye.

Mikhail Gorbachev was fourteen years old when the war ended. He would later describe its effect on him in his memoirs. "It has burned us," he would write, "leaving its mark both on our characters and on our view of the world."[1]

SCHOLAR AND STALINIST

After the war, Gorbachev resumed his schooling. A natural scholar, his favorite subjects were mathematics, physics, and literature. He also enjoyed acting in amateur theatrics. A committed Communist, he became secretary of the local Komsomol chapter. During the summers he worked with a government harvesting program. When he was seventeen, in recognition of his commitment and hard work, the government awarded him the Order of the Red Banner of Labour.

When he was nineteen, Gorbachev enrolled in the law school of Moscow State University. In 1952 he joined the Communist party. When Stalin died, he was part of the slow procession wending its way through the streets to view the open coffin. "I searched for traces of his greatness," Gorbachev would remember, "but there was something disturbing in his appearance which created mixed feelings."[2]

On September 25, 1953, Gorbachev was married to Raisa Maksimovna Titorenko, a postgraduate student of advanced Marxist-Leninist philosophy. Following his graduation from university, the couple went to live in Stavropol, a city not far from Gorbachev's home village. Here Mikhail became a Komsomol organizer, recruiting young people to communism.

ON THE FAST TRACK

Over the next several years, Gorbachev studied agronomy—the science of state-managed agriculture. In 1962 he was made a Communist party agronomist, charged with overseeing agriculture for the Stavropol territory. Besides his work with farm managers and workers, he was active in

Communist party affairs. By 1970 he was first secretary of the Stavropol region party committee. In this role he became a delegate to the Supreme Soviet. In 1971, at age forty, he joined the Central Committee of the Communist party of the Soviet Union.

Around this time Gorbachev met Yuri Andropov, then the head of the KGB. Andropov took Gorbachev under his wing. In 1978, Andropov was instrumental in Gorbachev joining the Secretariat of the Central Committee. Gorbachev was put in charge of directing national agricultural policy, making him one of the twenty most prominent officials in the USSR. He was not yet fifty years old, while most others in the highest echelons of the Communist government were in their seventies.

In his new position, Gorbachev initiated programs to increase Soviet food production, but they failed. Between 1978 and 1981, Soviet grain production fell by seventy-five million tons. Perhaps due to Andropov's backing, however, Gorbachev's career was not derailed by his failures. By 1984, with Andropov ill, there was much speculation that Gorbachev would replace him as the Soviet leader. However, the old guard preferred one of their own, and chose Chernenko. It was thirteen months more before Chernenko died and Gorbachev took over as general secretary of the Soviet Communist party.

STAR WARS AND DISASTER

Gorbachev took over with a commitment to perestroika and glasnost. He wanted to focus first on reform at home, rather than on detente and foreign policy. However, the Strategic Defense Initiative (SDI), President Reagan's missile shield nicknamed Star Wars by critics, demanded his attention.

The U.S. position was that SDI did not violate the 1972 ABM treaty. Gorbachev believed that it clearly did. He also understood that while SDI might protect the United States, it did nothing to protect America's European allies. In a speech that the United States understood as an attempt to split the western alliance, Gorbachev spoke of a "common European home."[3] He followed it up with visits to France and Great Britain. Prime Minister Margaret Thatcher of Britain, an outspoken anti-Communist, announced that the countries of the free world could do business with Gorbachev.

In November 1985, President Reagan and Gorbachev met in Geneva, Switzerland. They held six hours of private discussions. Reagan said that they "got very friendly," but the legitimacy of SDI was unresolved. Gorbachev said the USSR could build a better system. "Mr. President," he said, "you should bear in mind that we are not simpletons."[4]

Although the Reagan administration went ahead with SDI, Gorbachev declared a halt to Soviet nuclear testing. The United States refused to stop testing. Then something so terrible happened that these issues were shelved.

On April 26, 1986, there was an explosion at the Chernobyl nuclear power plant near Kiev in the Ukraine. Thirty-one people were killed immediately, and 135,000 people had to be evacuated from the area. Clouds of radioactive material spread over the European continent. The amount of radioactivity released was not known, its long-term effects impossible to assess. It was estimated that tens of thousands of people would eventually die of cancer. It was "the worst accident in the history of nuclear power."[5]

THE INTERMEDIATE NUCLEAR FORCES TREATY

Five months after the Chernobyl explosion, Gorbachev met with President Reagan in Reykjavik, Iceland. A deal limiting nuclear weapons fell apart when Reagan refused to postpone development of SDI. Each leader blamed the other for failing to compromise. Nevertheless, Soviet and U.S. negotiators continued to meet to hammer out details of a nuclear arms treaty. The result was the Intermediate Nuclear Forces (INF) treaty to be signed by Gorbachev and Reagan in Washington in December 1987.

Gorbachev's approval rating among Americans skyrocketed with news of the treaty. In a December 3 *New York Times*/CBS News poll, twice as many Americans viewed Gorbachev favorably as viewed him unfavorably. A solid majority said they believed he was succeeding in reforming the Soviet system. Two thirds supported the INF agreement.

The treaty was historic. Both sides agreed to demolish all their medium and short-range missiles. These included 1,752 Soviet and 859 American missiles and their nuclear warheads. For the first time, the two superpowers agreed to destroy existing weapons. Contrary to previous policy, the Soviet Union agreed to allow on-site inspections of its nuclear facilities.

At the White House in December 1987, Mikhail Gorbachev, left, and President Ronald Reagan sign the Intermediate-Range Nuclear Forces Treaty, which eliminated ground-based missiles of both nations.

Although the treaty eliminated less than 10 percent of the world's nuclear warheads, it was a key step toward total nuclear disarmament.

BOTHERSOME BORIS YELTSIN

Throughout 1987, perestroika and glasnost had been proceeding. However, as the Soviet people got a taste of freedom, their appetite for it grew. There were demonstrations and rallies in Soviet cities by Jewish refuseniks and other political dissidents demanding fewer restrictions and more reforms. There were complaints that Gorbachev was deliberately dragging his feet when it came to reforms. Chief among those making this charge was the first secretary of the Moscow Communist party, Politburo member Boris Yeltsin.

The same age as Gorbachev, Boris Yeltsin grew up in the village of Butka in a one-room cabin shared with five family members and a goat. He was regularly beaten with a belt by his father, a construction worker. Boris himself earned a reputation as a brawler. In one fight his nose was broken. In his youth he stole a hand grenade, which exploded and severed two fingers from his left hand. He drank vodka to excess, establishing a pattern of alcohol abuse, which would continue throughout his life.

Despite his wildness, Yeltsin graduated from the Urals Polytechnic institution as a civil engineer. In 1961 he joined the Communist party. By 1976 he was head of the party in Sverdlosk. In 1985, Gorbachev appointed Yeltsin to head the all-important Moscow Communist party. A year later Yeltsin was appointed to the Politburo.

In September 1987, Yeltsin became convinced that perestroika had reached a "critical phase."[6] By this he meant that the transition from proposals to action was too slow, that the impatience of the people was reaching the boiling point, and that those Gorbachev appointees who were responsible should be dismissed. He made these accusations at a meeting of the Central Committee of the Communist party on October 21.

Gorbachev reacted furiously. "What extreme egotism it must take to place personal ambitions above the interests of the party, above our common cause!" he raged.[7] He demanded that the Politburo accept Yeltsin's resignation as head of the Moscow party and as a member of the Politburo.

On November 3, Yeltsin wrote Gorbachev asking to be permitted to stay on as first secretary of the Moscow Communist party. Gorbachev refused. On November 9, at his office in party headquarters, Yeltsin was found covered in blood. He had evidently attempted suicide by stabbing himself with a scissors. On November 12, Boris Yeltsin was officially relieved of his duties.

DE-COMMUNIZING THE SATELLITES

One of Gorbachev's most far-reaching acts was his abandonment of the Brezhnev Doctrine—the right of the Soviet Union to intervene in the affairs of other countries militarily if they deviated from Communist doctrine—in March 1988. The previous month he had announced the withdrawal of Soviet troops from Afghanistan. The pullout from Afghanistan and the scrapping of the Brezhnev Doctrine energized the struggle for freedom in the satellite countries bordering the Soviet Union.

In 1989 the Hungarian parliament drew up a new constitution, ending the control of the Soviet-sponsored Hungarian Communist party. Radio Budapest announced the pullout of Soviet troops from Hungary. The Hungarian Communist party formally disbanded, changed its name to the Hungarian Socialist party, and adopted a program favoring democratic socialism over Marxism. In 1990, following free elections, a non-Communist government took over in Hungary.

That same year, anti-Soviet demonstrations swept over Czechoslovakia. The renowned author Vaclav Havel was sentenced to nine months in prison for inciting protests. After his release, the protests mounted. One after another of Czechoslovakia's Communist party officials was forced to resign. By the end of 1989, Vaclav Havel had been freely elected president of Czechoslovakia.

The pressures of glasnost were also felt in Poland. The ban on Solidarity was lifted. The Communist government negotiated an agreement on political and economic reforms with Solidarity and representatives of the Catholic Church. In June 1989 the first free elections in fifty years were held. Solidarity won overwhelming control of both the senate and the lower house. The following year, following sweeping economic reforms, Solidarity leader Lech Walesa was elected president of Poland.

THE WALL COMES DOWN

In Bulgaria the transformation from communism to democracy was slower. In May 1989 Todor Zhivkov, the Bulgarian Communist party chief who had been in power since 1954, announced a land reform plan for Bulgaria. Despite this, in December Zhivkov was forced to resign. The Bulgarian national assembly abolished the special status of the Communist party. It no longer would control the country's military and police forces. The Communist secret police were disbanded. In April the Bulgarian Communist party itself was disbanded. In June 1990, a free election was held.

Romania's liberation from communism was marked by bloodshed. Dictator of Romania since 1965, Nicolas Ceausescu had ruled by oppression and torture. Opposed to Gorbachev's peace efforts, he snarled that the West was "out to liquidate socialism."[8] In 1989 there were growing accusations that Ceausescu was responsible for ruining the Romanian economy. When protestors gathered in the Romanian city of Timisoara, Ceausescu's secret police opened fire on them. As the protests spread there were more shootings. Attempting to restore order, Ceausescu spoke directly to the public in the capital city of Bucharest. The event was televised nationwide. The boos and catcalls from his audience were so loud that Ceausescu was driven from the podium. The next day, when hostile crowds stormed Communist party headquarters, he and his wife fled. They were caught, tried by a military tribunal, and executed on Christmas Day 1989. A National Salvation Front was declared, and it decreed that Romania was no longer a Communist state.

The most dramatic reforms took place in East Germany. In October 1989, demonstrations in Leipzig against the Communist regime of East Germany attracted more than 300,000 people. When East German leader Erich Hoenecker ordered troops to fire on protesters, his ministers canceled the order and removed him from office. A few days later 500,000 anti-

Communists demonstrated in East Berlin. On November 7 the entire Communist East German cabinet resigned. The next day East Germany opened all of its borders, allowing free movement into West Germany. On November 9, a cheering crowd on both sides of the Berlin Wall watched as it began to be torn down. The following April, the first free elections were held in East Germany since the end of World War II. On October 3, 1990, East Germany was reunited with West Germany as part of the Federal Republic of Germany.

In East Germany, as in the other former satellites of the Soviet Union, perestroika had proceeded with astounding speed. Within little more than a year, the subject nations of the Soviet Union had rid themselves of Communist domination. But what of reform in the Soviet Union itself? Could Gorbachev really change the seventy-year-old structure of Communist rule inherited from the Bolsheviks and the Stalinists, and strongly supported by the old-line bureaucrats who still wielded power? Change itself wasn't the problem. The old-liners were. Could Gorbachev force change upon them, or would they take him down?

CHAPTER TWELVE

THE FINAL DAYS

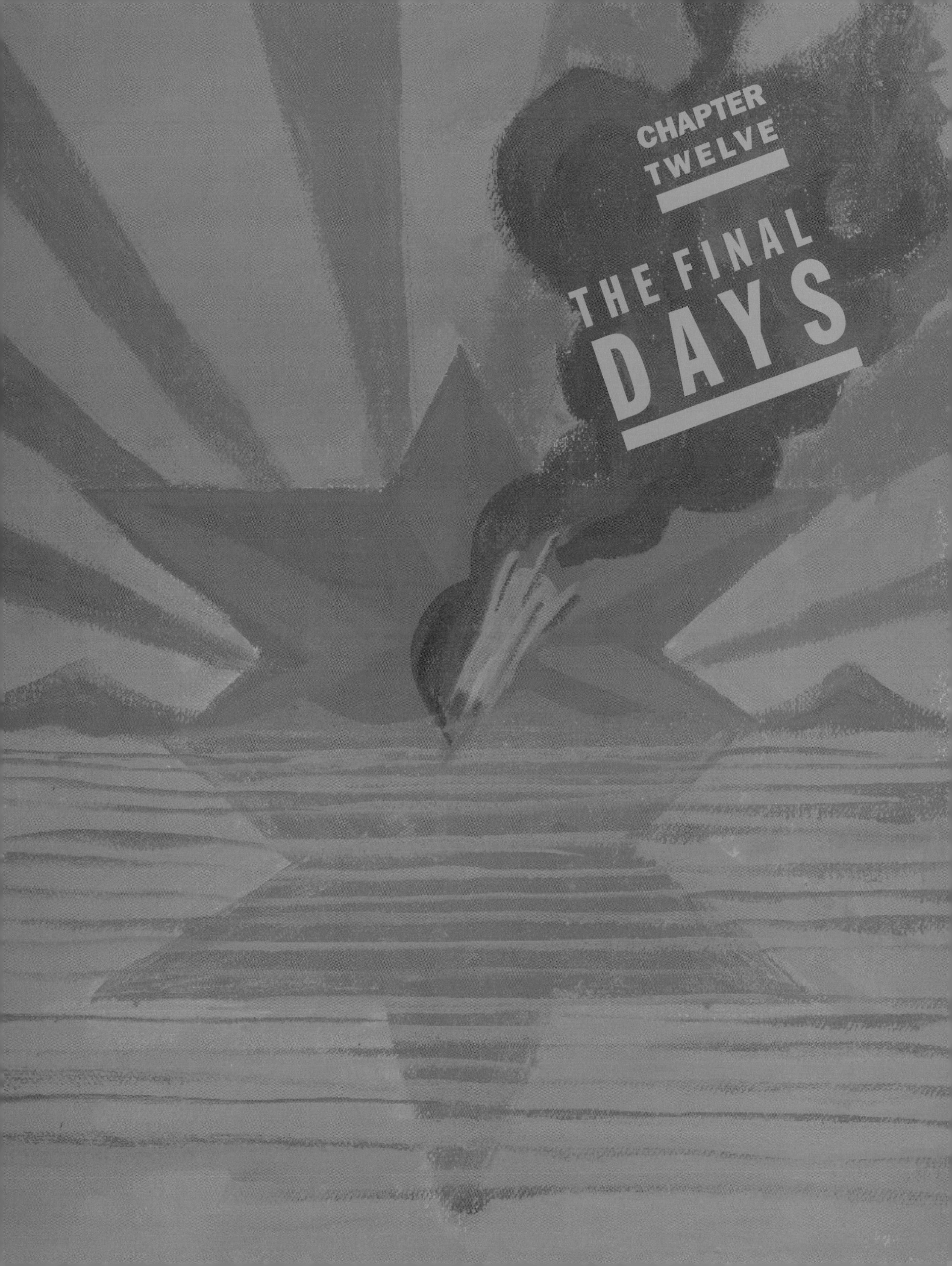

> *From the very beginning of the crisis brought about by the radical transformation of our society, I tried not to allow an explosive resolution of the contradictions to take place.*
>
> Mikhail Gorbachev

While the Soviet satellites were claiming their independence, Gorbachev was introducing reforms in the USSR. These included a new economic system based on the needs of the population, rather than solely on industrial and military growth. State-owned enterprises were given more freedom from central government control. These were allowed to make profits and to set wages accordingly. Market forces—a decidedly capitalist notion— rather than Soviet bureaucrats, were allowed to determine prices. There was a decentralization of trade, which had formerly been conducted under strict government supervision.

In October 1988, Gorbachev became president of the Soviet Union, thus firming up his hold on the government as well as the party. Two months later he addressed the United Nations and announced that he was reducing the Soviet military by 500,000 men. The problem was that the ailing Soviet economy had no jobs for these men. Also, hard-line Communists accused him of surrender to the United States. "Why did you lose Eastern Europe?" they demanded. "Why did you surrender Germany?"

Despite their opposition, a new constitution was adopted. Its major feature was a Congress of People's Deputies to be elected directly by the Soviet people. The first election to the congress, in which non-Communist parties were allowed to participate, took place in March 1989. Non-Communists won 20 percent of the seats. The greatest victory was scored by Boris Yeltsin, who had once again emerged as a spokesperson for speedier and more drastic reforms than Gorbachev was able to bring about. Yeltsin received six million votes, 89 percent of the total cast. Gorbachev, as head of the Soviet Communist party and president of the Soviet Union, did not have to run in the election.

THE GORBY SONG

Despite his power, as a reformer Gorbachev was subject to increasing pressures from opposing sides. The extremely popular Yeltsin kept speaking out for action rather than words. The old-line Communists threw up roadblocks to reform and accused Gorbachev of betraying Soviet Communist principles.

There was some truth to both positions. Because the USSR was so vast, and because conditions were so different in its fifteen Soviet Socialist Republics, reforms did weaken the power of the central government over the individual republics. On the other hand, the economic situation was worsening, and people were really suffering. In many parts of the USSR, the people were blaming Gorbachev with a song:

Sausage prices twice as high
Where's the vodka for us to buy?
All we do is sit at home
Watching Gorby drone and drone.[1]

Between 1989 and 1990, this discontent erupted in a series of miners' strikes in the Soviet Republics of Georgia, Armenia, and Azerbaijan. The miners demanded higher pay, shorter hours, and improved working conditions. In 1989 alone, these strikes resulted in 7.3 million lost workdays. When the strikers added political demands, the central government was forced to give up control of the mines. The loss of their income affected Gorbachev's already shaky ability to implement his reforms speedily enough to relieve the suffering of the people.

THE HUMAN CHAIN

Gorbachev's repudiation of the Brezhnev Doctrine revived ethnic and nationalist loyalties. There were demands for self-determination by the populations of some of the Soviet Republics. In the small Baltic Republics of Latvia, Lithuania, and Estonia, there was rebellion.

The Baltic Republics had been independent nations before World War II, when they were taken over by the Soviet Union by agreement with Nazi Germany, then its ally. Soviet power had kept them a part of the USSR for the next fifty years. On August 23, 1989, the fiftieth anniversary of the Nazi-Soviet pact, two million people formed a human chain across the three countries to demonstrate their demand for independence. Citing the rejection of the Brezhnev Doctrine, the Estonians called the Gorbachev era the "new awakening period."[2] Gorbachev at first sent troops to suppress the rebellions but later took a more conciliatory attitude, which eventually led to the republics' independence.

Trouble also broke out in the Ukraine. Ever since the revolution, many Ukrainians had resented Soviet rule. They considered it rule by the Communists of the Russian Socialist Republic imposed on Ukrainians. Soviet domination was particularly resented after the explosion at Chernobyl spread radioactive clouds over parts of the Ukraine. In November 1988 this resentment gave birth to the Ukrainian People's Movement for Restructuring (RUKH), which at first called for "sovereignty" and later demanded outright independence.[3] The movement grew and gained support throughout 1989.

The Chernobyl disaster was as devastating for the Soviet Republic of Belarus as for the Ukraine. Belarus was downwind of Chernobyl, and large areas of its farmlands were contaminated by nuclear fallout. There was an alarming upsurge in cases of childhood thyroid cancer and leukemia. The people of Belarus blamed the Soviet government.

ETHNIC AND RELIGIOUS CLASHES

Russification—the imposition of Russian language and culture on the non-Russian populations of the Soviet Union—was resented most strongly by the people of Moldavia. The Moldovans were a distinct ethnic group with strong ties to Romania. Since the end of World War II, in an effort to break those ties, the Soviets had blocked traffic across the Moldovan-Romanian border. With the advent of perestroika and glasnost, the Moldovans demanded an end to Russification. There were clashes with Russians living in Moldavia. In August 1989 the Moldovan parliament replaced Russian with Moldavian as the republic's official language. In 1990 the republic's name was changed from Moldavian SSR to the Moldovan SSR.

Perestroika and glasnost also awoke long-smoldering ethnic hostilities between the Soviet republics of Azerbaijan and Armenia. Azerbaijan's population was Muslim, Armenia's Christian. Religious clashes centered on the area of Nagorno-Karabakh. This area was originally Armenian, but in 1923 Stalin had made it part of Azerbaijan. By the 1980s, 85 percent of Nagarno-Karabakh citizens were Christian Armenians. Armenia repeatedly asked Soviet authorities for the return of Nagarno-Karabakh. They always refused, and Armenians and Azerbaijanis both believed that Gorbachev was biased in favor of Azerbaijan.

On February 27, 1988, when violence erupted, Gorbachev dispatched troops to the area. They were unable to restore order. Twenty-six Armenians and six Azerbaijanis died. Gorbachev worried that the situation was a "mine under perestroika." In December he met with representatives from the two republics and told them, "We are on the brink of disaster." In January 1990—following an earthquake in which 55,000 Armenians died—the fighting continued and Gorbachev again sent in troops and tanks. The Soviet soldiers killed 150 people, but again failed to restore order.[4]

There were also ethnic clashes in the Soviet republic of Uzbekistan in 1989 when fighting broke out between Uzbeks and the minority population of Meskhetian Turks. It resulted in over one hundred deaths. A battle between Uzbeks and Kyrgyz factions the following year ended with more than two hundred dead.

THE SEASICK SUMMIT

Pressured by the turmoil in the republics, as well as by the faction for speedier reforms led by Yeltsin, in August 1989 Gorbachev persuaded the

Politburo to authorize economic autonomy for the fifteen Soviet republics. This meant that they, rather than Moscow, could run their economies. The Supreme Soviet also passed a bill making strikes legal. No longer would wages, hours, and working conditions be subject to Soviet dictates.

While Soviet communism was loosening its hold on the republics, representatives of Gorbachev were meeting with U.S. negotiators in a series of Strategic Arms Reduction Talks (START). These resulted in a summit between Gorbachev and President George Bush in early December 1989. The meeting took place aboard a ship in the harbor at Malta during the worst storm to strike that island nation in five years. Flags were torn from masts and dinghies ripped loose from their moorings. Crossing from a U.S. cruiser to the Soviet liner in a small launch, President Bush and his aides were whipped by gale-force winds and drenched by sheets of rain. The Soviet ship, after they boarded it, was rocked by the high waves like an ill-balanced hammock. Reporters dubbed the meeting the "Seasick Summit."[5]

Despite the queasiness of the occasion, the two leaders got along well and made progress on a variety of issues. These included a trade agreement, completion of the withdrawal of Soviet troops from the countries of Eastern Europe, arms reduction, the destruction of stockpiles of chemical weapons, and the general reduction of armed forces in Europe. At the end of the meeting, Bush announced that "we stand at the threshold of a brand new era of U.S.-Soviet relations." Gorbachev enthusiastically observed that "[W]e buried the Cold War at the bottom of the Mediterranean Sea."[6]

GORBACHEV'S DECLINING POPULARITY

The year 1990 began with growing protests at the slow pace of reform in the Soviet Union. On February 3 hundreds of thousands of Russians marched through Moscow to demand an end to Communist domination. A month later the Congress of People's Deputies abolished the "leading role" of the Communist party in the Soviet Union.[7]

By midyear, Gorbachev's approval rating was at a new low. When he appeared at the Moscow May Day parade, he was loudly booed. Later that month, Yeltsin was made chairman of the Presidium of the Supreme Soviet of the Russian Federation. In effect, this made Yeltsin president of the Soviet Socialist Republic of Russia.

In August, Gorbachev briefly backed a plan drawn up by Yeltsin to bring about a free-market economy in the USSR. However, when he realized that the Yeltsin plan would undermine the basic structure of the Soviet Union, Gorbachev changed his mind. Yeltsin resigned from the Communist party in protest.

Yeltsin's resignation marked a sharp division between Gorbachev and the reformers. Other Yeltsin supporters including the mayors of Moscow and Leningrad also resigned from the party. On the other side, the old-line Communists opposed Gorbachev's foreign and domestic policies more and more strongly. Throughout the autumn of 1990, rumors that they were planning to overthrow Gorbachev swept through Moscow.

A TURN TO THE RIGHT

The one bright spot for Gorbachev was that in October 1990 he was awarded the Nobel Peace Prize for ending the Cold War. Even so, he could not ignore the threat of a plot to overthrow him. In an attempt to appease his conservative enemies, he appointed a number of those who had most stubbornly opposed his reforms to key positions in the government. Valetin Pavlov, who had been outspokenly hostile to Gorbachev's programs, was made prime minister. Soviet Foreign Minister Eduard Shevardnadze resigned in protest, warning that a dictatorship was coming.

Gorbachev's actions during the winter of 1991 seemed to confirm Shevardnadze's warning, but they were more likely a series of desperate efforts to retain power. Gorbachev removed pro-reform journalists from state television and radio. He saw to it that the streets of Moscow were patrolled by soldiers. He backed an effort to remove Yeltsin as head of the Russian republic by impeaching him. In Moscow on March 28, more than 100,000 people demonstrated in support of Yeltsin, and loudly denounced Gorbachev.

The political infighting continued. In March, Gorbachev had called for a nationwide vote confirming that the Soviet Union should be preserved "as a renewed federation of equal sovereign republics in which human rights and freedoms of all nationalities will be fully guaranteed."[8] Yeltsin persuaded the Russian republic parliament to add a clause to Gorbachev's proposal calling for the popular election of a Russian republic president.

Gorbachev's proposal was approved by 70 percent of all Soviet voters. Yeltsin's measure was approved by 85 percent of the voters in the Russian republic. The election for the Russian presidency was set for June 12 and Yeltsin easily won it. The Gorbachev-backed effort to remove Yeltsin from office had not only been defeated, it was now permanently prevented.

YELTSIN TO THE RESCUE

Persuaded by Yeltsin's victory, Gorbachev once again reversed direction. He spoke out for greater democracy, radical economic reform, and increased home rule for the Soviet republics. The hard-line Communists reacted. Prime Minister Pavlov requested that the Soviet parliament grant him emergency powers to initiate legislation and issue decrees without Gorbachev's approval. Gorbachev persuaded parliament to reject what he called this "constitutional coup."[9]

This only delayed things. In August 1991, while Gorbachev was on vacation in the Crimea, a State of Emergency Committee made up of high-ranking members of the government, military leaders, and KGB officials — all of whom had been appointed by Gorbachev—issued a declaration stating that he had been removed from power "for health reasons." Gorbachev was placed under house arrest at his vacation villa. A state of emergency was announced to "restore law and order."[10]

What happened next was perhaps the most dramatic incident in the struggle to shed Communist tyranny. Boris Yeltsin, the president of the Russian SSR, climbed atop a tank outside the parliament building in Moscow and denounced the State of Emergency Committee as illegal. Thousands of citizens filled the surrounding streets shouting their support of Yeltsin. They erected barricades against the armed forces of the hard-liners. When the committee ordered troops to storm the barricades, they refused. Some military units actually defended the protesting citizens.

On August 21 the troops withdrew. Yeltsin had the State of Emergency Committee members arrested. One of them committed suicide. On August

Boris Yeltsin, left, on a tank in front of Moscow's parliament building in August 1991, calls on the Russian people to resist the Communist hard-liners. Within months, the Union of Soviet Socialist Republics would cease to exist.

22, Gorbachev returned to Moscow and announced that he was back in charge of the government.

THE SOVIET UNION DISBANDS

Yeltsin, however, had not acted to restore Gorbachev's power, but rather to once and for all destroy the tyranny of the Communist party. He immediately suspended the activities of the Communist party in the Russian republic, and seized its property. When Gorbachev appointed new ministers to replace the traitors of the State of Emergency Committee, Yeltsin pronounced them unsatisfactory and forced acceptance of his own people instead. When Gorbachev addressed the Russian parliament, Yeltsin humiliated him with a series of interruptions.

Gorbachev could see that the tide of history was with Yeltsin. On August 24, while retaining his position as president of the Soviet Union, Gorbachev resigned as general secretary of the Soviet Communist party. Following Yeltsin's lead in the Republic of Russia, he disbanded the party's Central Committee and placed all its property under the control of the Soviet parliament. On August 29 the Congress of People's Deputies voted overwhelmingly to suspend all Communist party activities in the USSR. Gorbachev then made a last-ditch effort to preserve the Soviet Union, and his job as Soviet president. On September 5 he formed a new government composed of himself, the Supreme Soviet, and the presidents of the Soviet republics. The next day the new government recognized the independence of the Baltic nations of Latvia, Lithuania, and Estonia. By December one republic after another had declared their independence from the Soviet Union. In the Ukraine, 90 percent of the people voted for independence.

This did not go far enough for Yeltsin. On December 8, as president of Russia, he joined with the presidents of Belarus and the Ukraine in a decision to form a Commonwealth of Independent States (CIS). On December 21 eight other former Soviet republics—Moldova, Kazakhstan, Uzbekistan, Turkmenistan, Kyrgyzstan, Tajikistan, Armenia, and Azerbaijan—joined the CIS. Despite both having joined the CIS, Armenia and Azerbaijan continued fighting brutal battles over Nagorno-Karabakh for the next five years. While Georgia would join later, the three Baltic nations did not join the CIS.

On December 25, Gorbachev transferred control of the Soviet Union's nuclear weapons to Yeltsin and resigned the presidency of the Soviet Union. The next day the Supreme Soviet, the parliament of the Soviet Union, met and voted to permanently disband. On December 31, 1991, the Union of Soviet Socialist Republics formally came to an end.

AFTERWORD

"By any reckoning," observes History Professor Orlando Figes of Birbeck College, "the disintegration of the Soviet Union was one of the most astonishing events in modern history."[1] However, there were clear reasons for it. The Communist government had long tried to maintain a planned economy. It decided how much food to grow, what kind of goods would be manufactured, how much would be made available to consumers, what percentage of the national wealth would be siphoned off to train and arm the military, and more. From the start, the plans broke down and had to be replaced by other plans, which also eventually broke down. Droughts and war brought famine and suffering. After World War II, the people were forced to make sacrifices so that the nation could compete militarily with the United States. In the end, the economy failed to the point where chaos threatened.

To a large extent the failure was due to corruption and inefficiency within the system. Each ruler from Stalin to Gorbachev placed people in positions of authority who would put loyalty to their sponsors first, and commitment to the nation second. Every effort at reform was a threat to these functionaries. It didn't matter if they were true believers in Marxist-Leninist communism or self-seekers protecting their areas of power. The result was a roadblock to reorganization and change.

There were population shifts over the years, which also signaled the weakening of the Communist party's grip on the people. Millions of peasants moved from rural farmlands to the cities. By the 1970s the urban population outnumbered the rural population by two to one. Peasants had been more or less isolated from the outside world. In the cities their horizons widened—they sometimes saw foreign tourists, for example, and they encountered computers and other new technologies. Most significantly, millions of urban dwellers bought television sets. They glimpsed views of the Western world, of consumer goods, and a middle-class existence, which seemed both rich and exotic to them. The Soviet secret police were no longer able to seal off the population from capitalist culture and democratic ideas.

Gorbachev, although a committed Communist, saw that there had to be reform. He saw that the people were no longer unaware of the injustices of the Communist system. He saw that the point had been reached where if the government didn't act, the people would act for themselves. He instituted perestroika and glasnost over the objections of the old-line Communists.

However, when people taste freedom, the appetite for more freedom grows. The Soviet Union was made up of fifteen republics with a variety of nationalities, ethnic origins, and tribal affiliations. In many of these republics Soviet communism was regarded as the imposition of Russian authority. In the Russian Republic itself, Boris Yeltsin was insisting on reforms far beyond what Gorbachev was proposing. In the end, the alternative to communism, or chaos, was the independence of each of the republics.

From the beginning the Soviet system had not really worked. Whether socialism is a good or bad idea, the lack of democracy doomed it. The one essential to any system of government is a free society. For that reason more than any other, the fall of the Soviet Union was inevitable.

CHRONOLOGY

1945 — May — World War II ends in Europe.

August 6 — Atomic bomb is dropped on Hiroshima.

August 8 — The Soviet Union declares war on Japan.

August 9 — Second atomic bomb is dropped on Nagasaki.

August 15 — Japan surrenders to the United States and Great Britain.

September — War between the Soviet Union and Japan ends; American troops land in South Korea.

1946 — February — Stalin makes "Two Camps" speech declaring that peace is impossible until communism replaces capitalism.

March — Winston Churchill makes "Iron Curtain" speech in Fulton, Missouri.

1947 — Kim Il-Sung establishes Communist North Korean government with Soviet help.

1948 — March — United States launches Berlin airlift to bring food to Soviet-blockaded Berlin.

May — Free elections establish Republic of South Korea.

1949 — January — Communists complete takeover of China.

March — Stalin pledges military support to North Korean Premier Kim Il-Sung.

May—Soviets end Berlin blockade and United States ends airlift.

1950—June—Korean War begins as North Korea invades South Korea; U.S. troops enter war.

September—Soviets detonate first nuclear bomb.

October—Twelve Chinese divisions come to the aid of North Korea against U.S. troops; Soviets lend air support.

1952—Summer—Thirteen members of Jewish Anti-Fascist Committee are executed as Zionist spies.

November—So-called Doctors' Plot results in arrests of many prominent Soviet Jews.

1953—March—Joseph Stalin dies; hundreds perish in stampede at funeral; Georgi Malenkov succeeds Stalin as prime minister and first secretary of the Communist party; Malenkov resigns as first secretary, stays on as prime minister; Nikita Khrushchev takes over Malenkov's party duties.

June—East Berlin protest riots are put down by Soviet troops and tanks.

July—Cease-fire agreement ends Korean War.

August—Soviets detonate a hydrogen bomb.

December—Former secret police head Lavrenti Beria is executed.

1955—February—Malenkov resigns as prime minister; Nikolai Bulganin, backed by Nikita Khrushchev, replaces him.

May—The Warsaw Pact is formed by USSR and seven satellites.

1956—February—Khrushchev denounces Stalin and calls for "peaceful coexistence" with United States.

June—Polish workers riot; anti-Stalinist reformer Wladislaw Gomulka takes over Polish government and successfully resists Soviet pressure.

October—Hungarian anti-Communist rebellion is brutally put down by Soviets.

1957—October—Soviets launch *Sputnik*.

1958—March—Bulganin resigns; Khrushchev becomes premier as well as head of Communist party.

Summer—Khrushchev meets with Mao Tse-tung, pledges Soviet help to China in any conflict with United States.

December 31—Fidel Castro's rebel troops take over Cuba.

1960—May—Soviets shoot down U.S. spy plane piloted by Francis Gary Powers; Khrushchev-Eisenhower Paris summit collapses as a result.
October—Khrushchev throws shoe-pounding tantrum at the UN.

1961—January—Eisenhower administration severs ties with Cuba.
April—U.S.-sponsored invasion at Bay of Pigs in Cuba fails; Soviet's Yuri Gagarin becomes first human being in space.
August–September—Soviets build Berlin Wall between East and West Berlin.
October—U.S. and Soviet tanks and troops face off at Berlin Wall, but conflict is averted.

1962—July—USSR begins shipments of missiles and launchers to Cuba.
October—U.S. spy plane spots missile installations in Cuba; President John F. Kennedy informs nation; U.S. forces mobilize; Cubans shoot down a U-2 plane; Khrushchev agrees to withdraw missiles from Cuba and United States agrees to withdraw missiles from Turkey; Cuban missile crisis ends.

1962–1963—President Kennedy dispatches 17,000 troops as "noncombat advisers" to Vietnam to fight Communist Viet Cong rebels.

1963—August—Partial nuclear test ban treaty signed by United States, Great Britain, and USSR; as a result, Chinese denounce Soviets.

1964—August—Congress passes Gulf of Tonkin resolution authorizing President Lyndon B. Johnson to take any action necessary in Vietnam; Soviets increase aid to Vietnamese Communists.
October—Khrushchev is deposed; Leonid Brezhnev becomes first secretary of Communist party; Alexei Kosygin becomes Soviet premier; Chinese explode their first nuclear weapon.

1966—Spring—Chinese launch Great Proletarian Cultural Revolution.

1967—June—President Johnson and Premier Kosygin meet at Glassboro, New Jersey, and lay groundwork for future peace talks.

1968—April—Prague Spring begins with protests against Soviet control of Czechoslovakia.

August—Massive Soviet invasion of Czechoslovakia ends Prague Spring; Soviet troops remain in Czechoslovakia; Brezhnev Doctrine defines Soviet justification for interfering in affairs of other Communist countries; peace protests at Democratic National Convention in Chicago are put down by billy clubs and tear gas.

1969—March—Major border war erupts between USSR and China over Chenpao Island.
November—Strategic Arms Limitation Talks (SALT) begin in Helsinki, Finland.

1970—July—USSR-China border dispute is settled; relations between two countries improve.
December—Polish protests against high food prices results in dismissal of Communist party chief Wladislaw Gomulka; nine Soviet Jews convicted, two sentenced to death, in plane hijacking.

1971—February—Mass protest by Jews against Soviet government anti-Semitic regulations.
December—USSR and West Germany sign friendship treaty.

1972—May—President Richard Nixon and Leonid Brezhnev sign SALT I agreement in Moscow.

1979—June—President Jimmy Carter and Leonid Brezhnev sign Salt II agreement.
December—Soviet Union invades Afghanistan; Congress refuses to ratify SALT II; President Carter spells out Carter Doctrine and arms mujahadeen to fight Soviets in Afghanistan.

1980—August—Solidarity union formed by striking shipyard workers in Poland grows into national movement.
October—Kosygin resigns as premier of the Soviet Union.
December—Kosygin dies.

1981—January—Solidarity leader Lech Walesa is jailed.
December—Solidarity is outlawed.

1982—November—Leonid Brezhnev dies; he is succeeded by Yuri Andropov, former head of the KGB.

1983 — March — President Ronald Reagan announces Strategic Defense Initiative (SDI) in violation of 1972 ABM treaty.

August — Soviets shoot down Korean Air Lines flight 007, killing all 269 people on board.

1984 — February — Yuri Andropov dies; Konstantin Chernenko succeeds him.

December — Mikhail Gorbachev kicks off perestroika and glasnost in speech to Politburo.

1985 — March — Chernenko dies; Gorbachev replaces him.

November — President Reagan and Gorbachev meeting in Geneva, Switzerland, is friendly but not productive.

1986 — April — Explosion at Chernobyl power plant spreads nuclear clouds over Europe.

September — Reagan and Gorbachev meet at Reykjavik, Iceland, and blame each other for failure to reach agreement on eliminating nuclear arms.

1987 — September — Politburo member Boris Yeltsin tells Communist party Central Committee that perestroika is proceeding too slowly, and Gorbachev ministers responsible for this should be dismissed.

November — Yeltsin, removed from his posts, attempts suicide.

December — Intermediate Nuclear Forces (INF) treaty is signed by President Ronald Reagan and Gorbachev.

1988 — February — Gorbachev sends troops to end ethnic warfare between Armenia and Azerbaijan.

March — Gorbachev announces that the Brezhnev Doctrine is dead; Soviet troops begin withdrawal from Afghanistan.

October — Gorbachev becomes president of the Soviet Union after pushing through a new, more liberal constitution creating a Congress of People's Deputies to be elected directly by the people.

November — Ukrainian People's Movement for Restructuring (RUKH) is formed and demands sovereignty.

1989 — First Polish free elections since World War II are held; non-Communist government takes over in Hungary as Soviet troops pull out; Communist party government officials resign in Czechoslovakia and Vaclav Havel is elected president.

March—Boris Yeltsin elected to Congress of People's Deputies with 89 percent of the vote.

August—Two million people form human chain across three Baltic republics to protest Soviet rule; Moldovan parliament declares Moldavian, not Russian, the nation's official language; President George Bush and Gorbachev meet in "Seasick Summit" at Malta and declare end of Cold War.

1989–1990—Costly miners' strikes break out in Georgia, Armenia, and Azerbaijan.

1990—Lech Walesa overwhelmingly elected president of Poland; Bulgaria holds free elections; Romania declares it is no longer a Communist state; East Germany is reunited with West Germany to form the Federal Republic of Germany.

February—Mass protests by Soviet people because of slow pace of reform in USSR.

March—Congress of People's Deputies ends leading role of Communist party in Soviet Union.

May—Gorbachev loudly booed at May Day parade.

August—Yeltsin resigns from Communist party when Gorbachev refuses to back his economic plan.

October—Gorbachev awarded Nobel Peace Prize for ending Cold War.

1991—March—One hundred thousand citizens of Moscow demonstrate in support of Yeltsin and denounce Gorbachev.

June—Yeltsin is elected president of the Russian republic.

August—Hard-line State of Emergency Committee attempts to remove Gorbachev from power; he is held under house arrest; Yeltsin arouses the people in support of Gorbachev; members of the State of Emergency Committee are arrested; the coup is foiled; nevertheless, Gorbachev resigns as general secretary of the Soviet Communist party.

September—Gorbachev forms new, more democratic government, which recognizes independence of Latvia, Lithuania, and Estonia.

December—Eleven former Soviet republics, now independent, form Commonwealth of Independent States (CIS); Gorbachev resigns the presidency of the Soviet Union and transfers control of nuclear weapons to Yeltsin; on December 31, 1991, the USSR formally comes to an end.

CHAPTER NOTES

PREFACE

1. Nora Sayre, *Running Time: Films of the Cold War* (New York: The Dial Press, 1982), p. 97.
2. Howard Zinn, *Declarations of Independence: Cross-Examining American Ideology* (New York: HarperCollins, 1990), p. 259.
3. *Chronicle of the 20th Century* (Mount Kisco, NY: Chronicle Publications, 1987), p. 676.
4. *Chronicle*, p. 743.
5. Author Unknown, *How Can McCarthyism Be Explained?* Internet: www.social-studieshelp.com/Lesson_99_Notes.htm
6. *Chronicle*, p. 161.

CHAPTER ONE

Opening quote: Benjamin Frankel, ed., *The Cold War: 1945–1991, Volume 3* (Washington, DC: Gale Research, 1992), p. 56.
1. H. Montgomery Hyde, *Stalin: The History of a Dictator* (New York: Da Capo Press, 1971), p. 548.
2. Ronald Hingley, *Joseph Stalin: Man and Legend* (New York: McGraw-Hill, 1974), p. 393.
3. Hyde, p. 549.
4. Hyde, p. 551.

5. Hyde, pp. 551–552.

6. Ronald E. Powaski, *The Cold War: The United States and the Soviet Union, 1917–1991* (New York: Oxford University Press, 1998), p. 69.

7. Frankel, p. 57.

8. Powaski, p. 69.

9. *Chronicle of the 20th Century* (Mount Kisco, NY: Chronicle Publications, 1987), p. 619.

10. Jeremy Isaacs and Taylor Downing, *Cold War: An Illustrated History, 1945–1991* (Boston: Little, Brown, 1998), p. 50.

11. *Chronicle*, p. 637.

12. Alan Bullock, *Hitler and Stalin: Parallel Lives* (New York: Alfred A. Knopf, 1992), p. 860.

13. Bullock, p. 861.

CHAPTER TWO

Opening quote: Dmitri Volkogonov, *Autopsy for an Empire: The Seven Leaders Who Built the Soviet Regime* (New York: The Free Press, 1998), p. 160.

1. Volkogonov, pp. 152–153.

2. Volkogonov, p. 154.

3. Author uncredited, *Kim Il-Sung* NYPL Electronic Resources: Biography Resource Center, *Newsmakers 1994*, Issue 4, Gale Research, 1994, p. 1.

4. Author uncredited. *Kim Il-Sung, President of North Korea, 1948–*. NYPL Electronic Resources: Biography Resource Center, *The Cold War, 1945–1991*, Gale Research, 1992, p. 3.

5. Benjamin Frankel, ed., *The Cold War: 1945–1991, Volume 3* (Washington, DC: Gale Research, 1992), p. 64.

6. Volkogonov, pp. 157-158.

7. Volkogonov, p. 159.

8. Alan Bullock, *Hitler and Stalin: Parallel Lives* (New York: Alfred A. Knopf, 1992), p. 375.

9. Bullock, p. 956.

10. Abraham Brumberg, "On With the Show" (*The New York Times Book Review*, July 15, 2001), p. 18.

11. Bullock, p. 956.

12. Brumberg, p. 18.

13. Yakov Rapoport, *The Doctors' Plot of 1953* (Cambridge, MA: Harvard University Press, 1991), pp. 217–218.

14. H. Montgomery Hyde, *Stalin: The History of a Dictator* (New York: Da Capo Press, 1971), pp. 587–588.

15. Hyde, p. 588.

16. Hyde, p. 592.

17. Hyde, p. 592.

18. Hyde, p. 598.

CHAPTER THREE

Opening quote: Vladislav Zubok and Constantine Pleshakov, *Inside the Kremlin's Cold War: From Stalin to Khrushchev* (Cambridge, MA: Harvard University Press, 1996), p. 145.

1. Edward Crankshaw, *Khrushchev: A Career* (New York: The Viking Press, 1966), p.188.

2. Crankshaw, p. 189.

3. Jeremy Isaacs and Taylor Downing, *Cold War: An Illustrated History, 1945–1991* (Boston: Little, Brown, 1998), p. 126.

4. Zubok and Pleshakov, p. 144.

5. *Chronicle of the 20th Century* (Mount Kisco, NY: Chronicle Publications, 1987), p. 738.

6. *Chronicle*, p. 737.

7. *Chronicle*, p. 732.

8. Zubok and Pleshakov, p. 164.

9. Zubok and Pleshakov, p. 165.

10. Crankshaw, p. 191.

11. Crankshaw, p. 192.

12. Crankshaw, p. 193.

13. Crankshaw, p. 199.

14. Crankshaw, p. 200.

15. Crankshaw, p. 201.

CHAPTER FOUR

Opening quote: Nikita Sergeyevich Khrushchev, *Moscow speech, November 18, 1956* in *Bartlett's Familiar Quotations, Fourteenth Edition* (Boston: Little, Brown, 1968), p. 1032b.

1. Vladislav Zubok and Constantine Pleshakov. *Inside the Kremlin's Cold War: From Stalin to Khrushchev* (Cambridge, MA: Harvard University Press, 1996), p. 177.

2. Michael Kort, *Nikita Khrushchev* (New York: Franklin Watts, 1989), p. 87.

3. Author uncredited. *Nikolai Bulganin.* NYPL Electronic Resources: Biography Resource Center, *Encyclopedia of World Biography*, Gale Research, 1998, p. 2.

4. Kort, p. 60.

5. Kort, p. 76.

6. *Encyclopaedia Britannica* (Chicago: Encyclopaedia Britannica, 1984), vol. X, p. 555.

7. *Chronicle of the 20th Century* (Mount Kisco, NY: Chronicle Publications, 1987), p. 774.

8. Ronald E. Powaski, *The Cold War: The United States and the Soviet Union, 1917–1991* (New York: Oxford University Press, 1998), p.115.

9. Powaski, p. 115.

10. Powaski, p. 115.

11. *Chronicle*, p. 782.

12. *Chronicle*, p. 783.

13. Powaski, p. 116.

14. *Chronicle*, p. 787.

15. *Chronicle*, p. 807.

16. Edward Crankshaw, *Khrushchev: A Career* (New York: The Viking Press, 1966), p. 266.

17. *Chronicle*, p. 811.

CHAPTER FIVE

Opening quote: Michael R. Beschloss, *The Crisis Years: Kennedy and Khrushchev, 1960–1963* (New York: Edward Burlingame Books, 1991), p. 215.

1. *Chronicle of the 20th Century* (Mount Kisco, NY: Chronicle Publications, 1987), p. 818.

2. Dmitri Volkogonov, *Autopsy for an Empire: The Seven Leaders Who Built the Soviet Regime* (New York: The Free Press, 1998), pp. 231–232.

3. Jeremy Isaacs and Taylor Downing, *Cold War: An Illustrated History, 1945–1991* (Boston: Little, Brown, 1998), p. 171.

4. *Chronicle*, p. 831.

5. Volkogonov, pp. 232–233.

6. Volkogonov, p. 233.

7. Volkogonov, p. 234.

8. Benjamin Frankel, ed., *The Cold War: 1945–1991, Volume 3* (Washington, DC: Gale Research, 1992), p. 73.

9. Beschloss, pp. 217–219.

10. Beschloss, pp. 220, 223.

CHAPTER SIX

Opening quote: Jeremy Isaacs and Taylor Downing, *Cold War: An Illustrated History, 1945-1991* (Boston: Little, Brown, 1998), p.194.

1. Isaacs and Downing, p. 175.
2. Isaacs and Downing, p. 182.
3. Ronald E. Powaski, *The Cold War: The United States and the Soviet Union, 1917–1991* (New York: Oxford University Press, 1998), p 142.
4. Dmitri Volkogonov, *Autopsy for an Empire: The Seven Leaders Who Built the Soviet Regime* (New York: The Free Press, 1998), p. 236.
5. Volkogonov, p. 240.
6. Isaacs and Downing, p. 191.
7. Isaacs and Downing, p. 192.
8. Isaacs and Downing, p. 193.
9. Volkogonov, p. 242.
10. Volkogonov, pp. 243–244.
11. Volkogonov, p. 244.
12. Isaacs and Downing, p. 200.
13. Isaacs and Downing, p. 200.
14. Isaacs and Downing, p. 200.
15. Isaacs and Downing, pp. 202–203

CHAPTER SEVEN

Opening quote: Michael Kort, *Nikita Khrushchev* (New York: Franklin Watts, 1989), p. 145.

1. Ronald E. Powaski, *The Cold War: The United States and the Soviet Union, 1917–1991* (New York: Oxford University Press, 1998), p. 146.
2. Edward Crankshaw, *Khrushchev: A Career* (New York: The Viking Press, 1966), p. 284.
3. Kort, p. 131.
4. Benjamin Frankel, ed., *The Cold War: 1945–1991, Volume 3* (Washington, DC: Gale Research, 1992), p. 76.
5. *Chronicle of the 20th Century* (Mount Kisco, NY: Chronicle Publications, 1987), p. 904.
6. Powaski, p. 147.
7. Crankshaw, p. 286.
8. Dmitri Volkogonov, *Autopsy for an Empire: The Seven Leaders Who Built the Soviet Regime* (New York: The Free Press, 1998), pp. 254–255.
9. *Chronicle*, p. 925.

CHAPTER EIGHT

Opening quote: Author uncredited, *Alexsei Nikolaevich Kosygin, Prime Minister of the Soviet Union.* NYPL Electronic Resources: Biography Resource Center, *The Cold War, 1945–1991*, Gale Research, 1992, p. 4.

1. Ina L. Navazelskis, *Brezhnev* (New York: Chelsea House Publishers, 1988), p. 71.
2. Dmitri Volkogonov, *Autopsy for an Empire: The Seven Leaders Who Built the Soviet Regime* (New York: The Free Press, 1998), p. 273.
3. Author uncredited. *Alexsei Nikolaevich Kosygin*, NYPL Electronic Resources: Biography Resource Center, *Encyclopedia of World Biography*, 2nd ed., Gale Research, 1998, p. 1.
4. Volkogonov, p. 273.
5. Benjamin Frankel, ed., *The Cold War: 1945–1991, Volume 3* (Washington, DC: Gale Research, 1992), p. 76.
6. Ilya V. Gaiduk, *The Vietnam War and Soviet–American Relations, 1964–1973: New Russian Evidence.* From the Cold War International History Project (CWIHP) of the Woodrow Wilson International Center for Scholars, p. 2. Internet: http://cwihp.si.edu
7. *Chronicle of the 20th Century* (Mount Kisco, NY: Chronicle Publications, 1987), pp. 948, 952.
8. *Chronicle*, p. 960.
9. Frankel, p. 164.
10. Volkogonov, p. 283.
11. *Chronicle*, p. 981.
12. Frankel, p. 119.
13. Author's recording, August 1968.

CHAPTER NINE

Opening quote: Dmitri Volkogonov, *Autopsy for an Empire: The Seven Leaders Who Built the Soviet Regime* (New York: The Free Press, 1998), p. 321.

1. *Chronicle of the 20th Century* (Mount Kisco, NY: Chronicle Publications, 1987), pp. 999, 1005.
2. Geoffrey Hosking, *The First Socialist Society: A History of the Soviet Union from Within* (Cambridge, MA: Harvard University Press [second enlarged edition, paperback], 1996), p. 436.
3. Hosking, p. 437.
4. Benjamin Frankel, ed., *The Cold War: 1945–1991, Volume 3* (Washington, DC: Gale Research, 1992), p. 261.

5. Jeremy Isaacs and Taylor Downing, *Cold War: An Illustrated History, 1945–1991* (Boston: Little, Brown, 1998), p. 324.

6. Isaacs and Downing, p. 324.

7. Isaacs and Downing, p. 326.

8. Isaacs and Downing, p. 327.

9. Frankel, p. 123.

CHAPTER TEN

Opening quote: Ronald Reagan, *President Reagan's Speech to the British House of Commons, June 8, 1982.* Internet: www.luminet.net/~tgort/empire.htm

1. *Chronicle of the 20th Century* (Mount Kisco, NY: Chronicle Publications, 1987), p. 1183.

2. Jeremy Isaacs and Taylor Downing, *Cold War: An Illustrated History, 1945–1991* (Boston: Little, Brown, 1998), p. 330.

3. *Chronicle*, p. 1195.

4. Isaacs and Downing, p. 330.

5. *Chronicle*, p. 1212.

6. Isaacs and Downing, p. 342.

7. Ronald E. Powaski, *The Cold War: The United States and the Soviet Union, 1917–1991* (New York: Oxford University Press, 1998), p. 246.

8. Powaski, pp. 246–247.

9. Benjamin Frankel, ed., *Konstantin Chernenko, General Secretary, Soviet Communist Party, 1984–1985*, NYPL Electronic Resources: Biography Resource Center, *The Cold War, 1945–1991, 3 vols. Encyclopedia of World Biography*, 2nd ed. Gale Research, 1992, p. 2.

10. *Chronicle*, p. 1230.

11. Isaacs and Downing, p. 344.

12. *Chronicle*, p. 1235.

CHAPTER ELEVEN

Opening quote: Martin McCauley, *Gorbachev: Profiles in Power* (London: Pearson Education, 1998), p. 137

1. McCauley. p. 17.

2. McCauley, p. 20.

3. Benjamin Frankel, ed., *The Cold War: 1945–1991, Volume 3* (Washington, DC: Gale Research, 1992), p. 91.

4. *Chronicle of the 20th Century* (Mount Kisco, NY: Chronicle Publications, 1987), p. 1270.

5. *The World Almanac and Book of Facts: Millennium Collector's Edition* (Mahwah, NJ: World Almanac Books, 2000) p. 244.
6. McCauley, p. 70.
7. McCauley, p. 71
8. Jeremy Isaacs and Taylor Downing, *Cold War: An Illustrated History, 1945–1991* (Boston: Little, Brown, 1998), p. 396.

CHAPTER TWELVE

Opening quote: Author uncredited. *Mikhail (Sergeyevich) Gorbachev*, NYPL Electronic Resources: Biography Resource Center, *Contemporary Authors Online*, The Gale Group, 2001, p. 6.
1. Martin McCauley. *Gorbachev: Profiles in Power* (London: Pearson Education, 1998), p. 118.
2. Michael G. Kort, *The Handbook of the Former Soviet Union* (Brookfield, CT: The Millbrook Press, 1997), p. 83.
3. Kort, p. 57.
4. McCauley, p. 120.
5. Jeremy Isaacs and Taylor Downing, *Cold War: An Illustrated History, 1945–1991* (Boston: Little, Brown, 1998), p. 394.
6. Isaacs and Downing, p. 396.
7. Benjamin Frankel, ed., *The Cold War: 1945–1991, Volume 3* (Washington, DC: Gale Research, 1992), p. 46.
8. Ronald E. Powaski, *The Cold War: The United States and the Soviet Union, 1917–1991* (New York: Oxford University Press, 1998), p. 284.
9. Powaski, p. 286.
10. Powaski, p. 287.

AFTERWORD

1. Orlando Figes, "Who Lost the Soviet Union?" (*The New York Times Book Review*, January 20, 2002), p. 11.

GLOSSARY

Anti-ballistic Missile (ABM) Treaty—agreement signed in 1972 by the United States and USSR as part of the Strategic Arms Limitation Treaty (SALT I)

agronomy—the science of state-managed agriculture

Anadyr—code name for Soviet installation of nuclear missiles in Cuba

Baltic countries—Latvia, Lithuania, and Estonia

Bay of Pigs—body of water off the coast of Cuba where U.S.-backed invasion forces were defeated in 1961

Berlin airlift—U.S. Air Force campaign that flew food and supplies into Berlin on a daily basis when the Soviets blockaded the city in 1948 and 1949

Berlin Wall—six-foot-high stone wall topped by barbed wire and studded with gun positions and tank traps built by the Communists to stop people from escaping from East Berlin to West Berlin

blacklist—a list of names of alleged American Communist sympathizers compiled to drive them out of government, the entertainment industry, defense plants, educational institutions, media, and other areas

Bolsheviks—an early name for Soviet Communists

Brezhnev Doctrine—the right of the USSR to intervene in the affairs of other Communist countries if it deemed socialism to be in danger; proclaimed by Soviet head-of-state Leonid Brezhnev in 1968

Brezhnev era—the eighteen-year reign of Soviet leader Leonid Brezhnev, from 1964 to 1982

brinkmanship—a dangerously belligerent king of diplomacy

buffer zone—territories or nations forming a protective area between the USSR and potentially hostile countries

capitalist—in Soviet terms, a wealthy person who invests money to earn money in a free-market society

Central Committee—elite group of top Soviet Communist party officials elected at each party congress to act for the party as a whole

Checkpoint Charlie—only place where people could cross from West Berlin to East Berlin during the years the Berlin Wall was in place

Chernobyl—Soviet nuclear plant at which there was an explosion in 1986, sending clouds of radioactivity over Europe

Cold War—period between the end of World War II and the collapse of the Soviet Union marked by aggression and threats of aggression between the USSR and the free nations of the world

collectivization—ownership of land and other property by the state, rather than the individual

Commonwealth of Independent States (CIS)—Confederation of former Soviet republics formed in 1991 to replace the Union of Soviet Socialist Republics (USSR)

communism—theory of socialism that rejects all individual ownership

Communist party Congress—made up of members of Soviets and other Communist party organizations, the congress met roughly every five years to set goals and elect a new Central Committee, which in turn selected a new Politburo and Secretariat

Communist party of the Soviet Union—ruling organization in a one-party nation with complete power over the government

Congress of People's Deputies—congress created by the revised Soviet Constitution of 1988, composed of 2,250 members—two-thirds directly elected; the remainder selected by the Communist party and other Soviet organizations

Cuban Missile Crisis—U.S.-USSR confrontation when Soviets installed in Cuba nuclear missiles aimed at American cities; after coming to the brink of war, Soviet missiles were removed from Cuba in exchange for U.S. missiles being removed from Turkey

cult of personality—identification of a nation and its people with their leader

decentralization—redistributing power from the central Soviet government to the individual Soviet republics

detente—a lessening of tensions and hostilities between the USSR and the United States

Dnieper Mafia—Leonid Brezhnev loyalists from Dnepropetrovsk in the Ukraine

Doctors' Plot—Stalinist claim that Jewish doctors had plotted to kill high government officials

domino theory—belief underlying U.S. policy in Vietnam, which insisted that if the Communists won there, it would encourage rebellions throughout the rest of Southeast Asia and the Philippines, and that countries would fall to Communist aggression like dominoes

ExComm—Executive Committee of the U.S. National Security Council, which met to decide what action to take in the Cuban Missile Crisis

First Secretary of the Communist party—the most powerful person in the Soviet Union and, no matter who was premier, the actual head of the USSR government

glasnost—free dissemination of information and an end to secrecy at home and abroad

Great Fatherland War—name given to World War II by Soviet citizens

Great Proletarian Cultural Revolution—series of purges in China in the mid-1960s designed to remove from government and society at large all those whose ideas were opposed to those of Chairman Mao

guerilla—member of an underground organization fighting behind the lines in enemy territory

gulag—primitive prison camp usually set in a remote area

Gulf of Tonkin Resolution—passed by Congress following an attack on two U.S. destroyers in the Gulf of Tonkin off the coast of Vietnam—the resolution permitted the president to take aggressive actions without consulting Congress

ICBM—Intercontinental ballistic missile

imperialists—in Soviet terms, capitalist and colonialist empire builders

Intermediate Nuclear Force (INF)—accord signed in December 1987 that eliminated U.S. and USSR land-based nuclear missiles with a range up to 5,500 kilometers

Iron Curtain—Winston Churchill's term describing the line across Europe behind which dictatorship, secrecy, and lack of freedom characterized Soviet satellite nations

Jewish Anti-Fascist Committee—Jewish organization established during World War II to raise funds for the Soviet Union from non-Soviet Jews

KGB—Soviet secret police responsible for national security

Komsomol—Young Communist League of the USSR

Korean War—1950–1953 struggle in which Communist North Korea tried to take over South Korea, and the United States and China became involved on opposite sides. The war ended in a stalemate

Kremlin—seat of Soviet government

Leningrad—former Russian capital city; originally St. Petersburg, then Petrograd, now again called St. Petersburg

loyalty oath—pledge demanded by U.S. government and private business organizations, which employees signed to swear that they were not, and never had been, members of the Communist party or any organization which supported it

Marshall Plan—program devised by U.S. Secretary of State George Marshall to provide aid to enable the devastated countries of Europe to rebuild after World War II

Marxism-Leninism—principles of Soviet communism, named after Karl Marx and Vladimir Lenin

McCarthyism—named after anti-Communist right-wing senator Joseph McCarthy, a term applied to the harsh measures that tarnished innocent U.S. citizens and blurred the lines between liberals and Communists during the 1950s

MIRV—multiple nuclear warhead missile system

mujahadeen—Muslim fundamentalists financed by the United States to fight against the Soviet invasion of Afghanistan; also founders of the Taliban regime

North Atlantic Treaty Organization (NATO)—international defense force formed by Western democracies in 1949

NKVD—Soviet secret police

old guard—aging, but still powerful, Soviet leaders clinging in the 1980s to strict Stalinist-Communist doctrine; antireformers

partition—separating a country into two parts with two separate governments, as was the case with East and West Germany following World War II

peasant—farm laborer

perestroika—a reconstruction of the Soviet system to make it more democratic

Politburo—five-member panel appointed by the Central Committee of the Communist party to make quick decisions on urgent matters

Pravda—official newspaper of the Soviet Communist party

Presidium—another name for the Politburo

proletarian—lowest class of a society

purge—to dispose of political foes by exile, imprisonment, or execution

quarantine—term used for U.S. naval blockade that stopped and searched Soviet ships during the Cuban Missile Crisis

Reagan Doctrine—President Ronald Reagan's pledge to support "the forces of freedom in Communist totalitarian states"

Red Army—military land forces of the Soviet Union

refusenik—Soviet Jews who protested government policy preventing them from emigrating to Israel

reparations—payment to a government or an individual for damages suffered by the acts of an aggressor nation

Russification—imposition of Russian language and culture on the ethnic populations of the fourteen non-Russian republics of the USSR

Strategic Arms Limitation Treaty (SALT)—SALT I, limiting nuclear weapons, signed by the United States and USSR in 1979; SALT II was not ratified by U.S. Congress because of Soviet invasion of Afghanistan

satellite nations—countries whose policies are determined by another country, as in the case of the Soviet Union and the countries of Eastern Europe at the end of World War II

Seasick Summit—1989 meeting between Mikhail Gorbachev and President George Bush aboard storm-tossed ships in the harbor at Malta

Solidarity—Polish movement to unionize shipyard workers that eventually became a national political movement

soviet—council of workers

Soviet-German Non-Aggression Pact—1939 agreement by which Nazis and Communists conquered and split up Poland, and the USSR took over the three Baltic countries

Soviet Union—another name for the Union of Soviet Socialist Republics

space race—competition between the United States and USSR to make advances in the conquest of space

Sputnik—first man-made satellite launched into orbit, by the Soviets in 1957

Stalinism—Communism transformed into brutal one-man rule serving the power hunger of Joseph Stalin

Strategic Arms Reduction Talks (START)—negotiations between the United States and USSR on the reduction of strategic weapons systems resulting in 1991 START I pact and 1993 START II accord

Star Wars—nickname for President Reagan's Strategic Defense Initiative (SDI)

State of Emergency Committee—1991 old-guard Communists who attempted to overthrow Gorbachev

Strategic Defense Initiative (SDI)—President Reagan's plan to build an invincible missile shield

strategic nuclear weapons—missiles with nuclear warheads that can be fired from one continent to another

summit—meeting between superpower leaders

Supreme Soviet—parliament set up in 1936 and composed of two houses—Soviet of the Union and Soviet of the Nationalities—which often met in joint session, but had little actual power until the collapse of the Communist party in 1990–1991

tactical nuclear weapons—short- and medium-range nuclear missiles and other weapons for use in a specific territory being fought over

Third World—industrially backward countries not aligned with either the Communist or democratic bloc of nations

U-2—U.S. spy plane

Ukraine—non-Russian Soviet republic of farmlands and mineral resources

Union of Soviet Socialist Republics (USSR)—fifteen nations making up the Soviet Union

Viet Cong—South Vietnamese Communist guerillas backed by North Vietnam

Vietnam War—conflict throughout the 1960s and early 1970s involving North Vietnam (with military aid from China and the USSR), the Viet Cong, South Vietnam, and U.S. troops

Warsaw Pact—formed in 1955 and dissolved in 1991, a mutual defense agreement between the USSR and its Eastern European satellites

Zionists—Jews who fought to establish and maintain the State of Israel

FOR MORE INFORMATION

Crankshaw, Edward. *Khrushchev: A Career*. New York: The Viking Press, 1966.

Hosking, Geoffrey. *The First Socialist Society (Second Enlarged Edition)*. Cambridge, MA: Harvard University Press, 1992.

Kort, Michael. *Nikita Khrushchev*. New York: Franklin Watts, 1989.

Kort, Michael G. *The Handbook of the Former Soviet Union*. Brookfield, CT: The Millbrook Press, 1997.

Matthews, John R. *The Rise and Fall of the Soviet Union*. San Diego, CA: Lucent Books, 2000.

Navazelskis, Ina L. *Leonid Brezhnev*. New York: Chelsea House, 1988.

Powaski, Ronald E. *The Cold War: The United States and the Soviet Union, 1917–1991*. New York: Oxford University Press, 1998.

Volkogonov, Dmitri. *Autopsy for an Empire: The Seven Leaders Who Built the Soviet Regime*. New York: The Free Press, 1998.

Zinn, Howard. *A People's History of the United States*. New York: Harper & Row, Publishers, 1980.

Zinn, Howard. *Declarations of Independence.* New York: HarperCollins, 1990.

INTERNET SITES

The Baltic Republics of the Soviet Union: Estonia, Latvia, and Lithuania
http://depts.washington.edu/baltic/papers/sovietun.html

Radio Free Europe/Radio Liberty: Czechoslovakia in 1968: An Invasion
Remembered
www.rferl.org/nca/special/invasion1968/

Radio Free Europe/Radio Liberty: Ten Years After: The Fall of
Communism in East/Central Europe
www.rferl.org/nca/special/10years/

ThinkQuest: Fourteen Days in October: The Cuban Missile Crisis
http://library.thinkquest.org/11046/

Time 100 Polls: Leaders & Revolutionaries—Mikhail Gorbachev
www.time.com/time/time100/leaders/profile/gorbachev.html

INDEX